SMUGGLI
TRAILS

Cover: View from the Agglestone looking towards Poole Harbour

A view along Chesil Beach, looking towards Portland

SMUGGLERS' TRAILS

Pub Walks in Dorset

CAROL SHOWELL
& ROGER GUTTRIDGE

First published in 1997 by Red Post Books

A CIP catalogue record for this book is available from the British Library

ISBN 1-901533-00-X
Photography by Carol Showell and Roger Guttridge
Designed and produced by Crispin Goodall Design Ltd
Manufactured in the United Kingdom by Biddles Ltd

Red Post Books
463 Ashley Road
Parkstone, Poole
Dorset. BH14 0AX

Telephone (01202) 252144
Fax: (01202) 248370

Red Post Books *publish illustrated, non-fiction books. If you have a title which you think may be of interest, we would be pleased to hear from you. You should address your enquiry to the Editorial Director, at the above address.*

CONTENTS

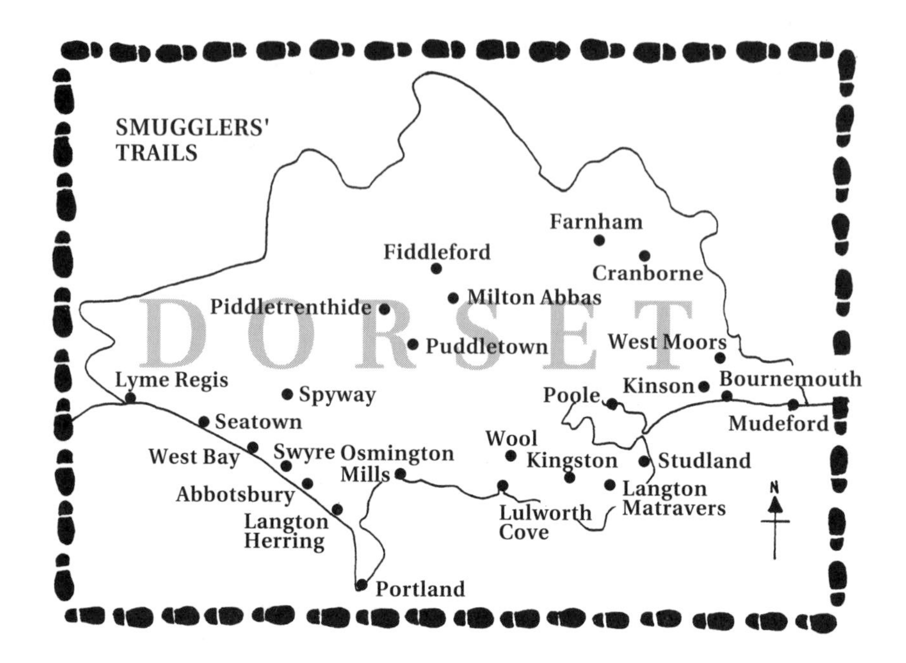

Smugglers' Trails: Pub Walks in Dorset began as an attempt to retrace the routes taken by smugglers as they carried their cargoes inland and then to develop them into a 'walking' book with a difference. Like the best-laid plans of many a smuggling gang and many a revenue officer, however, this plan too was destined to undergo a number of changes before it could come to fruition.

For obvious reasons, the smugglers of the 18th and early 19th centuries — the heyday of the trade in this country — left few records of their activities. As a result details of their routes are often unknown or unclear or can be pieced together only from odd scraps of evidence such as the names of roads and tracks (there are several Smugglers' Lanes and Paths in Dorset). Secondly, even when they are known, these routes rarely lend themselves to modern walks without major changes. Most walkers prefer circular routes but smugglers, of course, did not travel in circles! Their routes were designed to lead from A to B as quickly and securely as possible. What's more, they often do not coincide with the surviving footpaths and bridleways of today, making it difficult or impossible to devise walks based on them.

There are, however, many locations in Dorset which have a strong smuggling connection and it was these connections that provided the first criterion when devising the routes for the 25 walks in this book. Without exception, all can boast of having a great smuggling tradition — if not as a route used by smugglers then as a favourite haunt of smugglers or perhaps a site of some violent encounter between smugglers and government forces.

The second criterion was to identify smuggling-related locations which would also make interesting walks. In a county as varied and beautiful as Dorset, it must be admitted that this was not a difficult task! The coast alone provides an endless supply of interesting scenery and spectacular views and, given that there is hardly a stretch of coast which does not offer its share of smuggling tales, this aspect of the county features heavily in the choice of routes.

But the smugglers' work was not done when their cargoes reached the shores of England. For the land gangs whose job it was to convey the goods — mostly spirits, tea and tobacco — inland, it was just beginning. Much of the contraband was carried many miles to major towns and cities such as London, Bath, Bristol and even Worcester and the Midlands. For this reason many non-coastal locations also have their smuggling traditions, enabling us to select several walks among the hills, vales and heathland of inland Dorset.

Between them the walks pass through much of the finest scenery in Dorset — from stunning Heritage coast, unspoilt countryside and rich farmland to busy harbour, bustling town and tranquil village. There are walks for all moods and all weathers and there are walks of various lengths — from an easy stroll of 1.9 kms to a relatively challenging trek of 11 kms. Each has at least one pub associated with it and these too vary in character, from the snug country inn to the seaside bar to the star-rated hotel and restaurant. (Please note that while some licensees are happy for cars to be left in their car parks by walkers intending to use their premises, others have limited space and cannot offer this facility. Before setting out, consult the parking advice given in each chapter.)

Finally, while each walk has been tested at least twice and every effort made to provide accurate maps and directions, the authors and publishers cannot accept responsibility for the changes which inevitably occur from time to time — stiles removed, rights of way altered, gates erected, pub opening times varied. If you discover any changes, please send details to the publishers at Red Post Books, 463 Ashley Road, Parkstone, Poole BH14 0AX so that any future editions can be amended.

Happy walking!

KEY TO MAPS

Metalled Road
Footpath
Route
Woodland
Stile
Gate
Church
Signpost
Bridge
Camp site
Caravan site
Car park
Power lines
Telegraph pole
Milestone
Marsh
Golf course
Railway line
Barrier

Walk No: 1

THE SMUGGLERS' HEATH
Studland Heath-The Agglestone

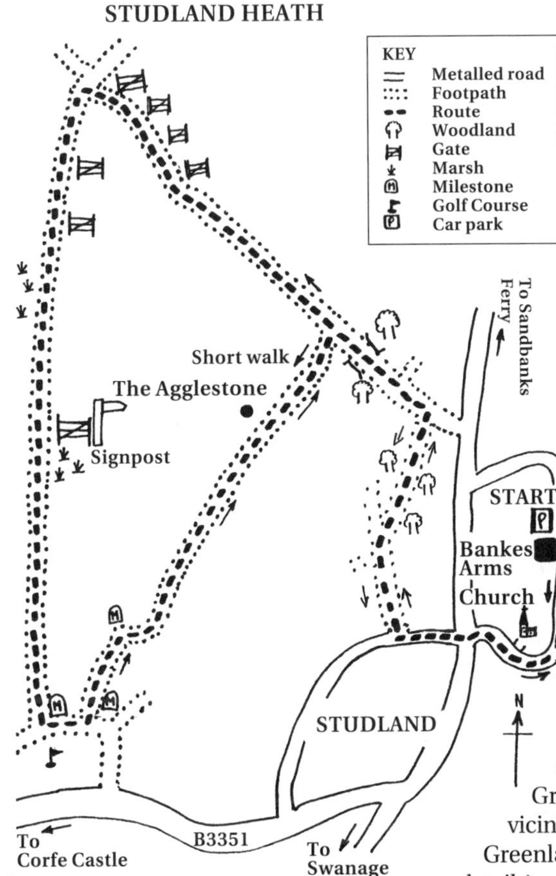

Distance: Longer walk 6 kms (4 miles); shorter walk 2 kms (1.5 miles).

Maps: OS Landranger 195 Bournemouth, Purbeck and surrounding area. Map ref: SZ 038 826.

Also, OS Outdoor Leisure 15 Purbeck.

Degree of difficulty: The walk offers good views almost from the start; by the time you reach the top of Godlingston Heath the views are spectacular. Both longer and shorter routes take in the famous Agglestone Rock. The going is marshy in one or two places, even in summer. There are gates but no stiles.

How to get there: Take the B3351 from Corfe Castle to Studland. As you enter the village, turn right at the first crossroads into School Lane. Turn left at Manor Farm, then follow the signs to the Bankes Arms. Alternatively, turn left at the crossroads into Heath Green Road and park in the vicinity of the bridleway sign to Greenland on the right (see walk details).

Parking: The Bankes Arms does not have a car park but parking is available in the National Trust car park next door. It is on the costly side in summer but free out of season.

Pub facilities: The Bankes Arms and its vast beer garden across the road overlook Studland Bay and boast unrivalled views across to Bournemouth, Hengistbury Head and beyond. The building became a pub in the 19th century, initially as the New Inn before adopting the name of the local landowning Bankes family around 1889.

The Bankes Arms is a family pub with a children's menu and a wide selection of meals. Local fish dishes are a speciality. A good range of drinks include six real ales. Accommodation is available in eight en suite rooms including a family room.

Opening times: Summer 10.30 am-11 pm Monday-Saturday (food 12 noon-9.30), 12 noon-10.30 pm Sunday; Winter 10.30 am-3 pm and 7-11 pm Monday-Friday, 1.30 pm-11 pm Saturday, 12 noon-10.30 pm Sunday (food daily 12 noon-2.30 pm and 7-9 pm). Tel: 01929 450225, fax 01929 450307.

Optional extras: A guide book on birds and/or heathland plants might be helpful to those with an interest in wildlife – this is nature reserve country with lots of species for spotters. Wellies are also recommended if it has been raining. Smoking is definitely not recommended, as heathland has a high fire risk, especially in dry weather.

Other attractions: Studland Beach. A fine, sandy shore, owned by the National Trust and popular among beach lovers and seaside strollers alike.

The Agglestone. A remarkable natural feature on Godlingston Heath (see History section for more details).

History: This is one for the walker who wants everything. Its views of the coast and heathland are second to none; so is its range of flora and fauna, hence the designation of much of the heath as a National Nature Reserve. With luck and a good eye, you could see (or hear) a Dartford warbler, one of Britain's rarest birds, or a smooth snake or sand lizard, the country's two rarest reptiles.

Surprisingly, the heathland itself is a man-made environment. It was created 4,000 years ago after Bronze Age farmers cleared large areas of poor quality woodland. The clearance upset the delicate balance which existed between soil and plantlife, creating even poorer acid soil where the most successful plant species are heather and bracken.

Godlingston Heath boasts one of Dorset's best-known natural landmarks, the Agglestone, which can be seen for miles around. According to local folklore, the Agglestone was hurled from the Isle of Wight by the devil, who was aiming for Corfe Castle but missed his target. The modern explanation is that both the Agglestone and its smaller neighbour, the Puckstone, on Studland Heath, are lumps of ferruginous sandstone which resisted the erosion that affected the softer material around them. The Agglestone is 18 feet high and 80 feet in circumference and is thought to weigh about 500 tons. Until the last century, ravens used it as a nesting site.

One and a half centuries ago this was prime smuggling country and at one time virtually every inhabitant of Studland village was a smuggler. The smooth sandy bed of Studland Bay and the gentle slope of the beach made for easier landings of contraband on moonless nights. On landing, tubs of spirits could be easily hidden under sand, bracken or piles of seaweed. Behind the beach deep-cut lanes and gorges, often shrouded in foliage, led inland across the heath. "When the smugglers carted

The Bankes Arms, Studland

the seaweed up on the land for use as manure, the tubs were carefully stowed away in the bottom of the cart and covered with seaweed," wrote the Swanage historian William Masters Hardy in his book on Purbeck smugglers, published in 1906. "At night they collected the booty and carried it down across the heath to Brand's Point, Greenland or Redhorn Quay. There it was put in flat-bottomed canoes and taken over to the other side of the harbour."

Studland's smuggling connections earned it a mention in several official reports over the years. As early as 1682 the Treasury investigator William Culliford – himself a Purbeck man – reported that smuggling vessels were anchoring in Studland Bay almost daily, landing some of their goods on Studland beach and taking the rest in "dragger boats" to Brownsea Island and later to Poole itself. His information came from John Tombs, a Studland mariner who admitted helping to carry goods ashore. For his trouble, Tombs was offered a job as a Customs boatman at £10 a year.

Reports from Poole Custom House a century later describe a bitter dispute between another Customs boatman, Thomas Hutchins, and Studland's smugglers, who resented his dedication to duty. Things reached a head in 1786 when Hutchins seized three casks of spirits from John Sinick, who retaliated by trying to break into Hutchins's house to get them back. When prosecuted for the break-in, Sinick responded by accusing Hutchins himself of buying smuggled tea.

A few days later the battle entered a new phase when Hutchins confronted Sinick and his wife on Studland beach and seized a cask of brandy from their canoe. Sinick wrenched back the cask, grabbed Hutchins by the collar, threw the boatman into the water and held-him under. Only the intervention of a passer-by saved the boatman from drowning. "After throwing up a consid-

The Agglestone

erable quantity of water, he recovered so far as to be able to come to Poole, which he immediately did, and came to this office with his clothes torn and very wet and with several marks of violence fresh on his body, which he had received in the affray," says the official report.

In another report dated 1804, Studland Bay was again named as one of Dorset's most popular contraband landing areas and in the 1820s cottages were built at Studland for members of the newly-formed Coastguard, whose main task was the prevention of smuggling. In 1841 25-year-old John Rolls, of Studland, a labourer, was jailed for six months at Dorchester for smuggling.

There have certainly been many smuggling runs in the area in modern times also, though we usually get to know only about those which are unsuccessful. These days, of course, cargoes are more likely to consist of drugs than spirits, tea and tobacco, although a major seizure at Shipstal Point in Poole Harbour in 1947 proved that there was still a market for contraband liquor at that time. The goods consisted of 1,236 mixed bottles, which were brought over from Cherbourg, transferred to a war surplus landing craft off the Isle of Wight, then landed at Shipstal and transferred again to a truck. But the locals became suspicious and police stopped the lorry before it reached Wareham.

The Walk: From the Bankes Arms, retrace your steps to the crossroads and go straight across into Heath Green Road. A little way after Heatherside on the right, turn into the bridleway marked Greenland.

Walk along the undulating track until you reach a footpath on the right, marked with a yellow arrow. It runs parallel to the track. When you reach a T-junction, turn left on the unmade lane.

After the cottage on the left, the path narrows and passes into a wood which in summer is fragrant with honeysuckle. After the bridge the path bears to the left and passes a National Nature Reserve sign on the right.

For the **shorter linear walk** to Agglestone, look out for a track on the left, which appears soon after you emerge from the trees. The path leads straight across the marshes and up some steps to the great rock itself. The views from here are quite exceptional. On a clear day you can see the Isle of Wight, the seven-mile stretch of beach from Hengistbury Head to Sandbanks, much of Poole Harbour and its islands and a considerable expanse of heathland. Enjoy the views and try to imagine the days when smugglers landed their goods on Studland beach, then made their way across the heath to Greenland, Brand's Point or Redhorn Quay, where the tubs of brandy would be transferred to flat-bottomed canoes and ferried to the northern and western shores of Poole Harbour.

When you are ready to leave the Agglestone, return by the same route.

For the **longer circular walk,** walk straight along the original track, which climbs through heather and gorse across rolling heathland. The path is now sandy and at the crest of the next rise Poole Harbour comes into view along with Sandbanks and Brownsea Island.

Ignore the tracks to the left and right and go straight on. At the next rise you will be able to see Shell Bay, Little Sea, Bournemouth and Poole.

Go through the gate, which bears a police warning to keep dogs on a lead, and across the grass. There is a short stretch between gorse bushes, followed by another gate, this time bearing a blue arrow.

Go through this gate and cross the next two fields diagonally to the right, using the wooden gate in the fence between them.

Turn left along the bottom of the meadow, go through the gate and cross a field. There is a marsh to the right. After the next gate the path leads diagonally to the left across the heath. There are no signs – just follow the track, keeping the fence to your right.

At the Swanage signpost, go through the gate and across the stones which have been laid over the marsh. If you look back you will be able to see the ferries berthed at Poole. To your right as you walk is a beautiful sweep of heath.

The path climbs, giving ever more stunning views. It is tempting to walk backwards to take advantage of them!

Keep walking, following the main track, and you will see the golf course on your right. At the milestone, walk on towards the Agglestone. The views remain breathtaking. On a clear day both Shipstal and Cleavel Points can be seen from here. It was at Shipstal in 1947 that 1,236 bottles of liquor were smuggled ashore before being seized at Wareham.

A little further on is another milestone. Here, turn left towards the Agglestone and the continuing views of Poole Bay and the Isle of Wight. The path goes downhill. At the next milestone turn left again and admire the view to Old Harry Rocks.

Follow the path to the Agglestone (clearly marked). You will probably wish to pause at this remarkable natural landmark but you are asked not to climb it.

When you are ready, continue past the stone and follow the track until you rejoin the original path, just before the wood. Then head back the way you came.

Walk No: 2

LIKE FATHER, LIKE SON
Seatown and Golden Cap

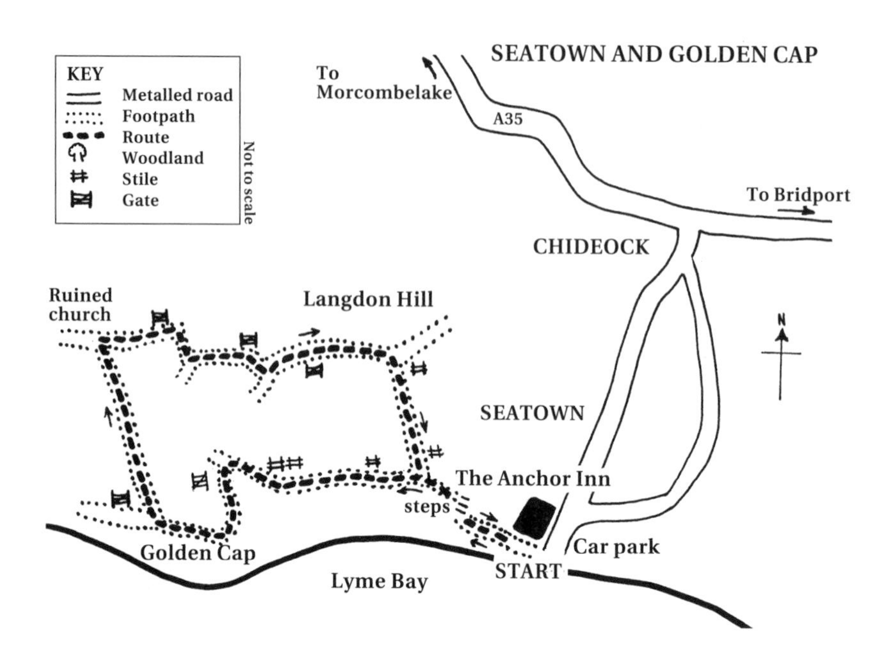

Distance: 5 kms (3.1 miles)

Maps: OS Landranger 193 Taunton and Lyme Regis. Map ref: SY 420 918.

Degree of difficulty: This is not a walk for the unfit, the unwell or the unhealthy, as the path to the top of Golden Cap is extremely steep! For those who are up to the task, however, the superb views from the summit make the hard climb worthwhile. The rest of the walk is easy and sheltered.

How to get there: Seatown lies due south of Chideock, reached via the A35 Charmouth-Bridport road. At Chideock, look for the Seatown turning near the church and follow the signs.

Parking: The Anchor Inn has a small car park for patrons but there is also a large car park opposite with an attendant who collects money in summer. There is no charge in the winter, when there is also on-street parking, as the double yellow lines do not apply.

Pub facilities: The Anchor Inn is open all year and has a family room. Bed and breakfast with rooms overlooking the sea is also available. The menu features a wide selection of hot and cold meals and snacks including local fish dishes and a children's menu. Food is served from 12 noon to 9.30 pm (Sundays 12 noon-2 pm and 6.30-9.30 pm Whitsun to September, 12 noon-2 pm and 7-9.30 pm September to Whitsun).

The Anchor Inn, Seatown

Outside is a large anchor acquired some years ago after being "caught" by a trawlerman between Moonfleet and Wyke Regis. It came from a Dutch ship wrecked on the Chesil Bank on January 16, 1748. The ship was bound for Amsterdam from Curacao with £50,000 worth of gold, silver and other valuables on board.

Fortunately for the crew, the foremast snapped as the vessel ran aground and they were able to use it to scramble to safety. Next day 200 locals could be seen digging in the pebbles for treasure; within a week an estimated 10,000 had joined the hunt!

A Portland man, Augustin Elliott, was subsequently tried for carrying away 10 ounces of gold and 20 of silver. After a long trial, he was acquitted. It was probably impossible to find a jury whose members were not involved in some way! The pub keeps a copy of the original account.

Opening times: 11 am-11 pm Monday-Saturday, 12 noon-10.30 pm Sunday. Tel: 01297 489215.

Optional extras: Binoculars, useful on any walk, are a must for this one, as the views from the top of Golden Cap are stunning. For the same reason the walk is best done on a clear day.

History: The extent of Seatown's involvement in smuggling is summed up in the writings of a Victorian curate of Chideock, the Rev T Worthington. "Within the memory of some of the inhabitants," he wrote in 1880, "there used to be from 30 to 40 fishermen at Seatown, ostensibly employed in their lawful avocations, but really in smuggling. Not the fishermen only, but as in other seaside places half a century ago, the inhabitants in general were implicated in this contraband traffic, of which the sin, in their eyes, consisted only in being found out. Numerous stories are told of hair-breadth escapes from the clutches of the Excise officers."

The smugglers of Chideock and Seatown had been at it a long time! Records of Quarter Sessions court hearings at Lyme Regis list no less than 18 men from the parish who were caught smuggling between 1724 and 1749 — more than Lyme itself and many more than for any other village in the Lyme Custom House area. The 18 included two members of the Peach family, two Farwells and four Ropers. Later records show that the Farwells at least were still smuggling a century later. Two Farwells were among the 28 Chideock and Seatown smugglers imprisoned at Dorchester between 1818 and 1841.

Another clergyman, the Rev C V Goddard, who was vicar of Chideock from 1890-95, also left notes about smuggling in his parish and identified the Farwells, Oxenburys and Bartletts (especially the Bartletts) as three of the leading families. The Oxenbury women used to carry tubs of spirits ashore hidden under their crinolines.

The Oxenburys also had a house at Roadstead Farm, where in the present century a secret room or chamber was discovered, formed between an external wall and an internal wall built for the purpose. Access was gained by removing floorboards in the room above. A similar chamber containing four casks of spirits was discovered by Customs officers at Chideock Mill in 1820. Such rooms were a common feature of smugglers' houses in many Dorset villages.

Chideock's churchwardens in Mr Goddard's time included a Sam Bartlett, who was raised in the smuggling business and had done little else since boyhood. Sam told Goddard that his father went to prison for smuggling after a cargo was found hidden in his orchard in north Chideock. Presumably he was one of the five Bartletts from the village listed in the Dorchester prison records for smuggling offences between 1821 and 1837. According to Sam, a Morcombe blacksmith was suspected of tipping off the revenue officials after overhearing smuggling talk in the Castle Inn. Nothing could be proved but there was reward money on offer and the blacksmith suddenly grew rich after Bartlett's capture.

Parson Goddard describes how smugglers brought cargoes of brandy across the Channel from the Bay of Seine in large boats. The vessels had extra gunwales, which could be slipped when at sea to enable kegs lashed together by rope to be thrown overboard and sunk in some well-marked spot until it appeared safe to land them.

"Then a number of men assembled (sometimes they borrowed a horse from a sleeping farmer, who in the morning fancied the fairies had been riding it, as it was so hot and tired), and carried the kegs off, ultimately selling them easily to farmers, gentry and even clergy."

Referring to the loss over the years of cottages at Seatown due to coastal erosion, Mr Goddard goes on: "The fishing interest seems to have slipped away with the dwellings. Some say the fish have left the coast, but others (with whom I agree) that in the old days the fishermen lived more by smuggling than by fishing.

"They were a hardy lot, and the son of one of them, himself engaged in the trade as a youth, recalls the smuggling yarns that he, as a little boy, used to hear them tell and the adventures in which later he took part. There were wild rushes to the West Rocks (beneath Golden Cap) when a boat-load of spirits was

Near Golden Cap

being rowed ashore from a ship lying out at sea, each man readily shouldering his share of the load — two small kegs — and scrambling off as fast as his legs could carry him. He would find his own way inland to a safe retreat. Cranborne Chase, being a wild uninhabited district, and the central moors of Dorset, were favourite hiding places."

Seatown beach was the scene of an incident in 1824 after Chideock coastguards Joseph Davy and John Rigler dared to scrawl a broad arrow on the hull of the *Fancy,* an alleged smuggling vessel from Seaton, Devon. The mark indicated that the ship had been seized but the smugglers, led by Robert and William Foss, had other ideas. "Damn your eyes!" said Robert Foss to Davy, holding his fist under his nose. "This'll be the worst day's work you ever did in your life." William Foss grabbed Davy by the collar and demanded to know what right he had to seize the boat. Then he held the officer captive until a team of horses which was to have been used to drag the boat back up the beach had left the scene.

According to Mr Goddard, Seatown's smugglers carried out their last run as late as 1882, and what a saga it was. It was led by the 69-year-old Sam Bartlett and began with the usual exchange of signals between the shore and a French ship hovering off the coast. But the initial landing at Eype's Mouth was punctuated by delays and mishaps. One smuggler was scarred for life after a colleague fell into him on the cliff; another drank himself to death on smuggled brandy. Only a few tubs were successfully landed before the Coastguard patrol was spotted. The rest were taken out to sea again and sunk off Seatown with weights and rope, to be collected at a later date.

Such was the diligence of the Coastguard by this time that it was months

The ruined church at Stanton St Gabriel

before another opportunity to land the goods presented itself. Even then the attempt at Burton Bradstock was hampered by heavy seas and again only a few tubs were landed. These were removed by waggon through a potato field but still half the original cargo remained at sea. A third landing was attempted below Thorncombe Beacon but the Coastguard were alerted, the boat's tackle got hitched and the tubs of brandy were once more dropped in the sea. Landing number four took place a few days later at Bridport Harbour but was again interrupted by the Coastguard, forcing the Seatown smugglers along the coast to Abbotsbury, where the last of the tubs were put ashore.

This walk also passes close to the ruined church of Stanton St Gabriel, reputedly used as a "receiving house for smugglers' kegs of brandy" after its closure in 1800. By this time Stanton St Gabriel was virtually a "lost village", abandoned by most of the families who had lived there for generations. These included the Gordge family, whose present-day Canadian descendant Trevor Lloyd believes they were involved in smuggling before their departure to nearby Charmouth in the mid-18th century. A note in the vestry minutes of St Matthew's Church, Charmouth, dated April 1765, suggests that not all the links with smugglers were severed even then. It refers to the commencement of a Customs prosecution against no less a person than the Parish Clerk Digory Gordge "on suspicion of aiding and abetting smugglers". But the note, signed by six individuals, adds: "We, thinking him quite innocent of the crimes alleged to his charge, and taking into consideration his poverty and his numerous family, do …… agree that we will assist him at the expense of the parish in making the least defence he is capable of doing."

The Walk: From the Anchor Inn, walk towards the sea and turn right on to the cliff path above the beach. Ahead of you is Golden Cap, a landmark for miles around and the highest cliff on the south coast of England.

The path turns away from the sea, climbs some steps and then turns left along the cliff again. A signpost points the way.

The next part of the walk is sheltered by bushes and bracken. On the right is a footpath signposted Chideock and Langdon.

Carry straight on, following the Golden Cap sign.

At the wooden stile follow the sign marked Charmouth three and a half. The route crosses an exposed piece of grass, where the few trees and bushes are bent away from the sea by the onshore wind.

Golden Cap rises ahead, looking bigger and steeper by the minute! To the left is the sea, with views to the south Devon coast.

Begin the steep climb to the top, and when you need to stop, use the time to look at the view unfolding behind.

Just before the top is a very welcome seat, where you can rest and admire the scenery. Far below can be seen the roof of the pub, people looking like ants on the beach and the coastline sweeping east towards Chesil and Portland.

When your legs have recovered, cross the stiles (two of them side by side) and walk straight on. You will now have a view to the north west and be able to see the A35 trunk road as it passes through Morcombelake, where the famous Dorset Knob biscuits are made.

Go through the gate on the left and follow the stepped path through the scrub to the top of Golden Cap.

At the triangulation point you are at a height of 191 metres with a breathtaking 360 degree view.

When you are ready, follow the path across Golden Cap and walk down the steps to the gate. You will have a clear view of Lyme Regis across the bay.

From the gate, head straight across the field towards the ruined Church of St Gabriel which you can see before you. There is a seat here for those who wish to enjoy the tranquil atmosphere.

At the bottom of the hill, with the church ruins on your left, turn right and walk along the track away from the church, keeping the hedge on your left.

Go through the five-bar gate and bear right, following the bridleway and footpath sign. Walk up the slope, again keeping the hedge on your right.

At the next signpost walk in the direction of Langdon Hill. Cross the field to the next gate and turn right, following the edge of the field and the sign to Langdon Hill. There is a fence on the right. (NB Although the official footpath follows the perimeter of the field, some walkers may be tempted to use a direct route across the field — in which case the next sentence is irrelevant.)

It is only a short way to the next signpost, where you turn left towards Chideock and Seatown.

At the wooden gate walk straight on, again signposted Seatown/Chideock. The path is sheltered and pleasant, with glimpses of the sea to the right.

When you reach a stile on the right, climb over, and head towards the sea. You will be able to see the cliff path ahead of you, reached by either of two stiles. Climb one of the stiles and walk back to the car park.

Walk No: 3

THE PIRATES' PORT
Poole Park and the Quay

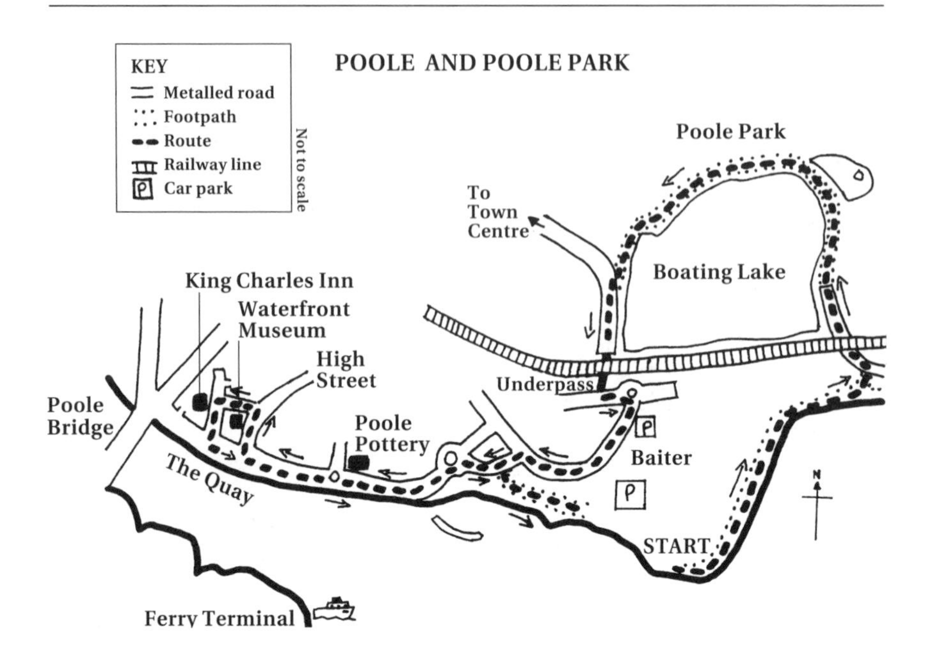

Distance: 5 kms (3.1 miles).

Maps: OS map 195 Bournemouth, Purbeck and surrounding area.
Map ref: SZ 020 903.
Estate Publications red street plan (Bournemouth).

Degree of difficulty: This is an easy walk on level ground but allow plenty of time, as there is much to see and do. There are no stiles, gates or steps anywhere on the route, making it especially suitable for pushchairs and wheelchairs.

How to get there: On reaching Poole, follow the signs to the Quay, then to Baiter.

Parking: There is a large pay and display car park at Baiter, an area of largely reclaimed land east of Poole Quay.

Pub facilities: The King Charles Inn in Thames Street is one of several historic pubs on and around Poole Quay and is one of the finest and oldest not only in Poole but in Dorset. It dates back to 1550 and was a popular haunt of smugglers. It was originally called the New Inn and owes its present name to King Charles of France, who landed at Poole Quay after fleeing his own country. Features include some ancient-looking beams, probably old ship's timbers. The upstairs bar — available for functions but open to the public only at selected times — retains slightly more of the olde worlde atmosphere and overlooks the old Poole

Custom House, built in 1813 and now a popular cafe-bar.

The King Charles is a Whitbread pub offered two real ales and reasonably priced bar meals and snacks including "healthy and hearty" traditional brown baps with a wide choice of fillings. The menu includes a couple of vegetarian options and a children's menu. Children are welcome in the restaurant area until 9 pm.

Opening times: 11 am-11 pm Monday-Saturday, 12 noon-10.30 pm Sunday (food 12 noon-9.30 pm Monday-Thursday, 12 noon-6 pm Friday-Saturday, 12 noon-5 pm Sunday). Tel: 01202 674950.

Other pubs on or close to the Quay include **the Helmsman, the Portsmouth Hoy, the Poole Arms, the Jolly Sailor, the Lord Nelson** and **J J Murphy's Stout bar.**

Other attractions: Poole Park has a boating lake, miniature train and cafeteria.

Poole Quay is a magnet to visitors and locals alike and has something for everyone. It's a place where the old blends well with the new as museums, potteries and historic pubs rub shoulders with restaurants, takeaways and souvenir shops. In summer boat trips are available to Brownsea Island, around the harbour and beyond.

Major attractions around the Quay include the **Waterfront Museum**, set in the medieval Town Cellars and five-storey Oakley's Mill, built in the 18th century. Pirates and smugglers feature in its many displays. Tel 01202 683138.

Also on the Quay are the **Aquarium Complex** (tel 01202 686712) and **Poole Pottery,** billed as "the south's most famous pottery" (tel 01202 666200).

The King Charles Inn, Poole, once a favourite haunt of smugglers

For further information contact the **Tourist Information Centre**, also sited on the Quay (tel 01202 253253).

Optional extras: A bag of bread or scraps will help the wildfowl population to entertain you as you pass the lakes in Poole Park.

History: Poole's natural harbour — the second biggest in the world — has given it a great maritime tradition and, inevitably, a long association with pirates and smugglers. Its reputation as a place of wrong-doing even gave rise to the following doggerel, which could be recited in every household for miles around:

If Poole were a fish-pool,
and the men of Poole fish,
There'd be a pool for the
devil and fish for his dish.

Poole's most famous pirate was Harry Pay. He was born within yards of the High Street and lived here in the late 14th and early 15th centuries. The Spanish called him "Arripay", a knight who "scours the seas as a corsair, with many ships, plundering all the Spanish and French vessels that he could meet with". In 1406 the French and Spanish took revenge with a dawn attack which reduced much of Poole to a smouldering ruin. There were casualties on both sides and the dead included a brother of Harry Pay. But the pirate himself was away at sea and his own house was among the few which escaped the fire.

Almost three centuries later, in 1682, a Treasury investigation uncovered widespread corruption among Poole's Customs officers and evidence of 19 separate smuggling incidents involving large quantities of tobacco, wine, brandy, cloth and other goods. Investigator William Culliford named former mayors John Carter (who was also a magistrate) and Moses Durrell as leading figures in the contraband trade. Carter imported cargoes of wine, brandy, spices, linen and whalebone and "did a great trade, mightily advancing it by the several intrigues he uses in defrauding the king and the nation".

Much of the contraband came ashore at Baiter, which was a dark and lonely spot in the 17th century. The only buildings were a windmill and stable and the latter was regularly used for storing contraband. Carter and Durrell had even built some steps at the water's edge to make life easier for their contraband carriers as they came ashore. Around the town itself, they had a network of helpers and hiding places, including sheds, haylofts, cellars and secret rooms. Carter's men were usually armed with swords and clubs and disguised by masks and women's tall hats. "Many Customs officers have felt the weight of these clubs and never been able to discover the persons that gave it," an informer claimed.

Culliford took various measures in an attempt to curb the smuggling trade in Poole but it appears to have continued almost unabated as soon as his back was turned. By 1720 it was so rife that the town's leading citizens begged for Government help on the grounds that it was damaging legitimate trade. Measures were again taken but then they complained that even more damage was being caused by the numerous prosecutions!

Poole Quay was the scene of a famous incident in 1747 when 30 smugglers from Kent and Sussex tied up a nightwatchman and broke into the Customs warehouse to recapture their cargo of tea. They included members of the notorious Hawkhurst Gang from Kent, who were among the most ruthless criminals in the land. The raid was successful but some of the gang were eventually tracked down and hanged after murdering a witness and the Customs officer escorting him to give evidence against them.

Beneath Poole Quay and parts of the old town is a network of drains and underground passages which in the past proved invaluable to smugglers. During

The former Poole Custom House, built in 1813

a high tide or after a heavy downpour, they could float a line down the passage from an inland access point to its mouth at the Quay, where accomplices would attach items of contraband to be hauled back up. On drier occasions the men themselves sometimes crawled along the tunnels to emerge with their goods in some old inn or cellar.

One drain or tunnel known to have been used by smugglers opened into the harbour near the Fish Shambles on the Quay. Another ran under Caroline Row and emerged at its upper end at the Baker's Arms. This old inn has since been demolished but other buildings associated with smugglers survive, including the King Charles (formerly the New Inn), once a favourite haunt.

The character of old Poole, with its cobweb of narrow streets and alleys lined by an assortment of buildings from many centuries, made it relatively easy for smugglers to conceal contraband once it was landed. "Poole proved a town of innumerable hiding places," write the late historian Bernard Short. "Not a house was to be found that had not its secret storing place, its corner of mystery where the stranger might not intrude."

One of the few buildings which presumably does not have its secret hiding places is the elegant Custom House on the Quay, built in 1813 after fire destroyed its 18th century predecessor. Outside is the old King's Beam, the official scales once found in front of almost every custom house in the land.

The Walk: Park at Baiter (not forgetting to buy a ticket) and head east along the path which follows the water's edge. Poole is a working port as well as a tourist resort and there is always something interesting to watch.

The path offers unrivalled views across Poole Harbour and its shipping lanes, where cargo vessels and fishing boats come and go and great cross-Channel ferries dwarf dredgers, pilot boats, yachts and pleasure craft.

In the past thousands of smugglers used these shores and waters. A few still do, although these days their cargoes are likely to be of a less romantic kind, such as drugs or firearms.

The scenery is excellent, with Brownsea Island in the near distance, the Purbeck Hills and Corfe Castle beyond.

A stretch of the path runs parallel to the Weymouth to Waterloo railway line. Where the railway track bears left and goes into a cutting, walk across the grass and turn left on to the road.

As it passes under the railway bridge, the road reduces to single width. But there is a narrow footpath on one side.

With the boating lake on your left, pass through the pillars marking the entrance to Poole Park. On the right is another, smaller lake, home to many varieties of hungry waterbirds), a cafe and – in summer – a miniature train.

Where the road divides, turn left, pass the war memorial, and follow the edge of the lake.

As you approach the railway line you will see Park Lake Road immediately on your right. The road is a cul-de-sac leading to a subway under the railway, which links Poole Park with the reclaimed land at Baiter.

Go through the underpass, sparing a thought as you do so for the poor fellows who devoted Christmas Day 1971 to its construction – the only day in the year when there were no trains running!

After emerging from the underpass, turn right on to the pavement which leads into Catalina Drive.

Follow the road back to Baiter and on towards the Quay. The route is sign-posted.

Just before the Quay are the moorings for fishing boats. There is always something interesting to watch here. There may be a boat out of the water or being painted, or perhaps a fisherman mending his nets.

Just beyond the boats is the RNLI Old Lifeboat House, which opens to the public in the summer season and has a small souvenir shop. Poole also has the national headquarters of the RNLI in nearby West Quay Road.

Whatever the weather or season, there is always lots happening on the Quay. Permanent attractions include Poole Pottery on the right, which opens to the public, as does the Purbeck Pottery further along.

At the bottom of the High Street is the Waterfront Museum, a major and relatively recent addition to the Quay's growing list of attractions.

The next side road off the Quay is Thames Street where the timbered King Charles Inn can be found.

Before returning to Baiter, you may wish to walk a little further to the end of the Quay for a look at the lifting bridge, which opens from time to time to allow larger vessels to pass through.

Walk back along the Quay, looking out for all the interesting things which you missed the first time. There are sure to be some!

If you have worked up an appetite or a thirst, there are pubs, restaurants, take-aways and snack kiosks to satisfy every taste and pocket.

As you walk along the Quay, remember that beneath your feet are the old drains which provided the route to shore for many illicit cargoes.

Walk No: 4 'I NEVER WAS A SMUGGLER BEFORE' Abbotsbury and Abbotsbury Castle

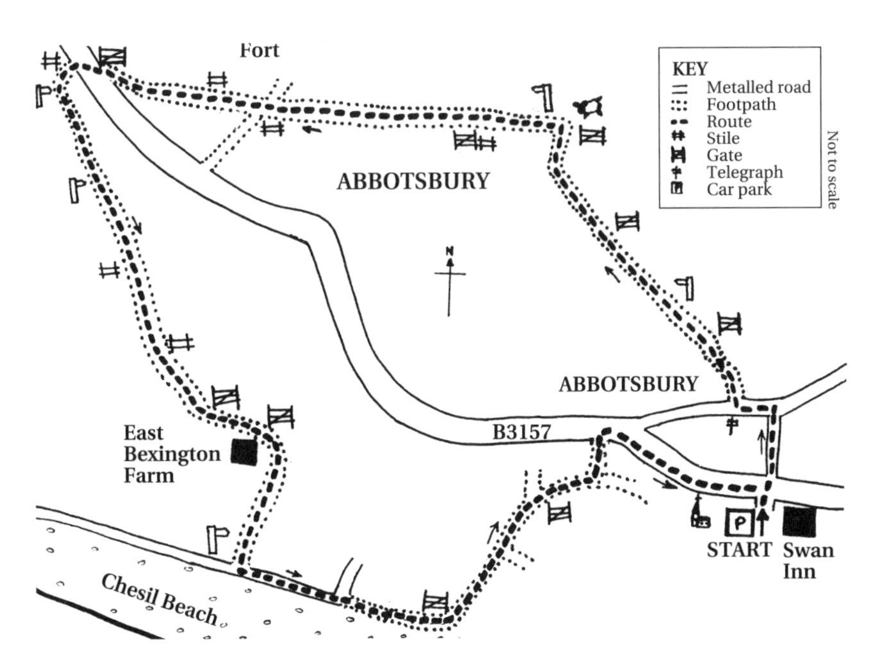

Distance: 9.6 kms (6 miles)

Maps: OS Landranger 194 Dorchester, Weymouth and surrounding area. Map ref: SY 579 853.

Degree of difficulty: There is a fairly steep climb from the village of Abbotsbury to the hill fort. The walk is planned so that the steepest part, from the fort to the beach, is downhill. The section between the B3157 and Chesil Beach can be muddy at times.

The walk takes in a variety of scenery — from upland to coastal — and is full of interest. The views from the hills are superb, giving a spectacular panorama over Lyme Bay and the villages north west of Abbotsbury. The view to the south — over the Fleet to Portland — is reminiscent of an aerial photograph. To make the best of the walk, therefore, choose a clear day.

The first part of the walk is not well marked, so particular care has been taken with the map and directions.

How to get there: Abbotsbury is on the B3157 midway between Bridport and Weymouth. The Swan Inn and public car park are at the eastern end of the village, on the main road. The car park is signposted from the village.

Parking: The Swan Inn has a large car park opposite. There is also a large public car park (with charges) next door to te pub. Walkers are welcome to use the pub car park providing they are also using the pub before or after their walk.

Pub facilities: With his surname and a local ancestry, it would not be a surprise if Graham Roper, landlord of **The Swan Inn,** were to claim descent from local smugglers! In fact, he has no knowledge of such a connection but it is no secret that few local families were more entrenched in the contraband trade than the Ropers of South West Dorset — the name appears no less than 11 times among the smugglers listed in the records of Dorchester Prison and the Lyme Regis Quarter Sessions.

The Swan is a family pub and restaurant with an extensive menu, including children's menu, and a selection of wines. Facilities include a children's room with games and rides, a patio and garden with swings and a traditional red telephone box called a "Playphone"! The children's room can also be converted to a skittle alley.

Opening times: Summer 10.30 am-11 pm seven days a week; out of season 11 am-3 pm and 6-11 pm (but can open all afternoon for parties booking in advance). Tel: 01305 871249.

The Ilchester Arms Hotel in Market Street, Abbotsbury, is an old coaching inn and more than two centuries ago was reputedly the local headquarters of the great Dorset smuggler Isaac Gulliver. It's now a Greenall Premier hotel with extensive menu, nine bedrooms, beer garden and car park at the rear. Tel: 01305 871243.

Optional extras: Camera and binoculars. Warm clothing on a windy day, as the wind whistles on the upland.

Other attractions: Abbotsbury has more than its share of attractions, including a prehistoric hill fort, 18th century subtropical gardens, the site of a Benedictine monastery founded by Orc, steward to King Canute, and a famous swannery dating from the 14th century, when the monks reared swans for food. Other survivors of the monastic era include the Great Barn and, on a hilltop overlooking the sea, St Catherine's Chapel, where spinsters have traditionally made a pilgrimage to pray for a husband. In Abbotsbury's Church of St Nicholas is a Jacobean pulpit bearing two bullet holes acquired during a Civil War encounter 350 years ago.

Visitors are well catered for at Abbotsbury, where teashops and craft and souvenir shops abound.

History: In November 1720 a group of fishermen from Abbotsbury made an unusual catch a mile off the Dorset coast and set off a remarkable chain of events which culminated in a question in the House of Commons. The catch consisted of 23 barrels of brandy and two barrels of wine which had been "moored with ropes to stones" and sunk in the sea, obviously by smugglers, who often used this method intending to return to collect their goods later. In this case the stuff was taken to the home of Whitteridge, the Abbotsbury Excise officer, only to be "re-seized" on behalf of the Lord of the Manor, Thomas Strangways, who claimed it as a manorial perk.

A veritable tug-of-war followed with Whitteridge and his young Customs colleague, Joseph Hardy, recapturing the goods, only to give them up again in response to intimidation by the Abbotsbury mob. In the end the cavalry was sent for and the mob found themselves

The Swan Inn, Abbotsbury

facing 19 troops from Lord Irwin's Regiment of Horse as well as revenue officials and the parish constable. This time the seizure was successfully completed, though Strangways made such a fuss that questions were subsequently asked in the House and the Secretary at War received a complaint about the involvement of troops in such matters.

By 1720 Abbotsbury already had a reputation as a smuggling village, and a rough one at that. Three years earlier Joseph Hardy's predecessor Benjamin Hounsell received a severe beating at the hands of the smugglers, led by John Maynard, "a fellow of some substance, the most concerned in the smuggling trade of any man in those parts and the chief person in this offence". Maynard was charged and tried for beating and wounding Hounsell but acquitted. Two years later poor Hounsell met a tragic end after attempting to ride from Bridport to Abbotsbury through the sea. He was found badly injured on the shore after being thrown by his horse and trampled, and afterwards "continued senseless and died".

Abbotsbury was the scene of many other smuggling incidents down the years, some of them involving circumstances which were less than straightforward. In 1736 Customs man William Randell seized a large quantity of jewellery, cloth, silk and satin products from a stall at Abbotsbury Fair. They had been offered for sale as "run goods just arrived from Guernsey" but turned out not to be contraband at all but items made in England. The tactic, presumably, was a ploy to increase their appeal by making out they had been illegally imported! Such was the popularity of British goods.

Some of the cargoes landed hereabouts were extremely large. In April 1737, 1,500 pounds of tea were found hidden in hedgerows at Bexington together with quantities of brandy, rum, silk, cotton and handkerchiefs. The tea was in 53 oilskin bags, two of which were

The Ilchester Arms, Abbotsbury

in a mackerel pot. Officials concluded that the contraband was to have been taken to London by fish-carriers who took mackerel to the capital every year at this time.

In 1743, following a desperate chase at sea, a crew of smugglers scrambled ashore at Abbotsbury with a cargo which included 990 pounds of tobacco, 200 pounds of tea, 16 gallons of brandy and five gallons of rum. Unfortunately for them, they were immediately met by Customs riding officer Edward Thorne and were "so harried, weary and confused that they could not escape him". Thorne gratefully laid claim to the entire haul and the bonuses that implied.

Generations of Abbotsbury smugglers made good use of the Fleet and its sheltered waters. "The mode of smuggling carried on in this district is by means of sinking small casks of spirits in the Fleet or backwater, getting them up as opportunity offers," reported another Abbotsbury officer, Benjamin Brown, in 1815. The smugglers also made use of the road leading to the botanical gardens founded by Lord Ilchester in the 18th century. It became known as Smugglers' Walk.

From the records of Dorchester Prison, it is clear that Abbotsbury's smugglers remained active until the middle of the 19th century. Twelve of them appear in the records between 1817 and 1843 (including William Roper in 1843), and for every smuggler caught we can be sure there were many more who remained at large.

Among those listed is a young Abbotsbury basketmaker, Moses Cousins, who was caught carrying four gallons of brandy in 1832 — a time of depression and great hardship for the working people of England. Cousins, a married man aged 23, had been trying to supplement his meagre income with a little smuggling and from his prison cell wrote a pathetic plea to the local squire Lord Ilchester in the hope of obtaining an early release. "I never was a smuggler before," he says in a letter which survives in the Dorset Record Office. "But as trade being dull, and being introduced to convey that little quantity of spirits for the sake of a few shillings, as times being hard owing to family afflictions, that I has been very much reduced." Cousins goes on: "The gentlemen of Abbotsbury can certify they never knew me in the act of smuggling before, till

View north of Abbotsbury

this time, and I solemnly declare never to be guilty of the like offence, in which I am greatly oppressed under the sentence of mind on the account of the loss of my business and the sorrowful distress of my wife." Cousins' plea appears to have been successful for he was released from prison within 17 days of sending the letter having served just 60 days of what would normally have been a 12-month sentence.

The Walk: Turn into the lane opposite the entrance to the public car park, next to the Swan Inn. East Farm House stands on the corner.

Walk 29 up the hill to the end of the lane, then turn left into Hands Lane. Look out for Spring Cottage, a thatched house on the right, and turn into the lane immediately past it on the right. The lane is unmarked but there is a telegraph pole opposite the entrance and lots of walkers' bootprints in the soil!

The steep track passes a thatched cottage called Copplestone on the left, before leaving the houses behind and becoming an ancient sunken track.

The path goes between bushes, then bears right up the hill. To the left is a good view over the village with the Fleet beyond.

The track continues to climb, giving views across to St Catherine's Chapel on its hill.

Go through the gate marked with a blue arrow and the track will then open out. At the wooden signpost go straight on. The way is not signposted but the land is under the Countryside Stewardship scheme.

Follow the track across the downs to the gate. There is a blue arrow.

Go through, and continue straight on up the hill to another gate.

Go through this gate also, and follow the signpost marked Hill Fort. The track goes across rough grass with rocky outcrops and grazing sheep.

The path heads diagonally to the left and is still uphill.

At the top you are on the edge of the

ridge, with Chesil Beach and the sea to your left.

Head towards the signpost, and follow the sign to West Bexington.

After the next gate and stile — marked with a blue arrow — you will be on top of the downland with a stupendous panoramic view over the whole of the Fleet to Portland.

The path runs beside a wire fence on the right, behind which are some tumuli. This part of Dorset is rich in prehistoric settlements.

Pass beneath the power lines on to a wide grassy stretch. There are views of the sea to the left and of distant villages to the right. Ahead can be seen Wears Farm and behind it the hill fort.

The path goes under two more power lines before reaching a stile just before the road that runs between the fort and the main road.

Climb the stile and the fort is immediately to your right. Cross the access road and follow the track up the bank.

At the top is a beacon erected by West Dorset District Council on the spot where one was lit 400 years ago to warn of the approach of the Spanish Armada in 1588.

Cross the stile marked with a yellow arrow and follow the track along the ridge. It leads down on to a grassy field. Head across the field towards the main road. There is a gate ahead, in the corner where the stone wall meets the fence. Once through the gate, there is a verge and a safe place to cross the road to the stile opposite.

Climb over the stile, marked with a yellow arrow and National Trust acorn. This is Tulk's Hill, National Trust land. Follow the path alongside the dry stone wall on the left. Look behind you for a good view of the hill fort.

At the end of the stone wall, turn left, following the signpost to Chesil Beach. The path leads downhill, between bushes. At the next signpost carry straight on towards Chesil. Cross the next stile and walk straight down the field.

Cross the stile at the bottom of this field and you will find yourself halfway down another. Follow the track diagonally down the field towards the farm.

Go through the gate and the farm will be on the right, complete with Second World War pillbox.

A little way further on is the next gate. Go through the gate and follow the track as it curves to the right, passing around the farm.

Continue straight down the field towards the sea. At the time of writing, the farmer had left a grassy strip on the right for walkers.

Turn left on to the narrow access road, following the sign to Abbotsbury. The beach is immediately to the right.

At the junction with the Abbotsbury road on the left, go straight on past the car park. There are some Heritage Coast information boards on the right.

Continue along the shingle path. There is a sheltering hedge on the left. Go through the gate and straight on.

The path turns away from the beach, giving your last view of the Fleet.

Follow the sign to Abbotsbury and, where the gravel track bears right, go through the gate marked with a yellow arrow and follow the route indicated.

Follow the main track back to the village.

When you reach the road, turn right on to the pavement and head back to the car. You will pass several tearooms and craft shops on the way.

Walk No: 5 THE SMUGGLERS OF FIDDLEFORD MILL
Fiddleford and Sturminster Newton

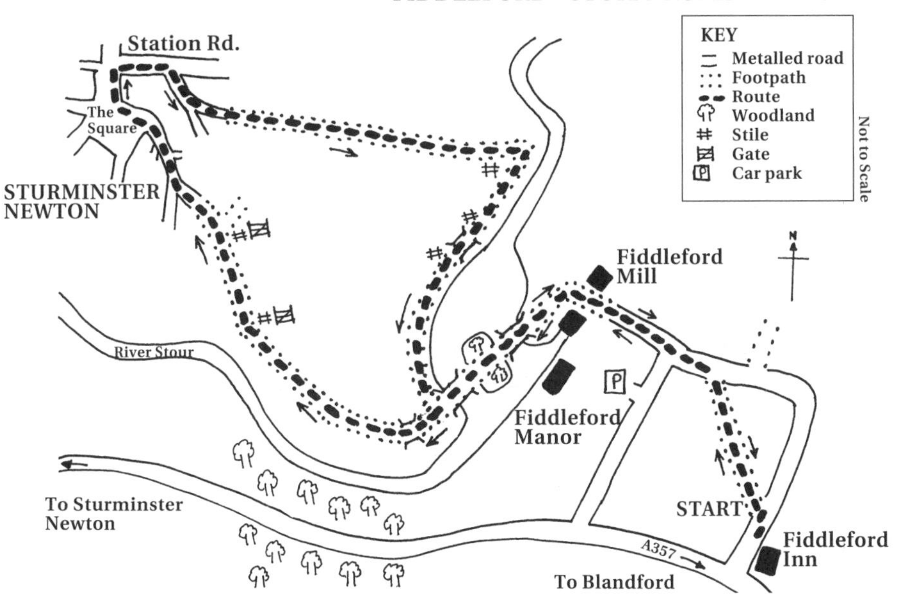

Distance: 5 kms (3.1 miles)

Maps: OS Landranger 194 Dorchester, Weymouth and surrounding area. Map ref: ST 805 132. (The route uses official footpaths which may not be marked on your OS map.)

Degree of difficulty: This is a very pleasant walk with a few stiles but no steep hills. Much of the route is across water meadows — no idle term — and waterproof footwear is advisable in all but the driest weather.

How to get there: Fiddleford is a scattered hamlet beside the A357 road less than two miles south-east of Sturminster Newton. The Fiddleford Inn is a few yards from the main road — turn off at the sharp steeply-banked bend.

Parking: The Fiddleford Inn has a car park for patrons but please ask permission before setting out, especially at weekends. If the car park is full or unavailable, we suggest parking either in the lane outside or half-a-mile away in the Fiddleford Mill and Manor car park (map reference 802 136) which also lies on the route.

Pub facilities: The Fiddleford Inn is a pleasant and popular free house serving a wide range of home-cooked food using mostly English recipes.

The extensive menu includes at least three vegetarian choices and six or seven

The Fiddleford Inn

specials each day. There are also good selections of wines and beers including four real ales. Meals are served in the bar, dining room and in the large beer garden beside the Darknoll Brook. The garden has children's swings but the favourite attraction, at the time of writing, is a fox tame enough to relieve its fellow customers of their leftovers!

Contrary to some published sources, the Fiddleford Inn was never a pub before the late 1960s, when it opened initially as the Archway House Hotel. It was, however, a brewery in the 18th and 19th centuries and features in the legends of Roger Ridout the smuggler.

Opening times: Summer 11.30 am-2.30 pm, 6.30-11 pm Monday-Saturday, 12 noon-3 pm and 6.30-10.30 pm Sunday; Winter 11.30 am-2.30 pm, 6.30-11 pm Monday-Saturday, 12 noon-3 pm, 7-10.30 pm Sunday. Tel: 01258 472489.

Other attractions: Fiddleford Manor, next to the redundant mill, is one of the oldest manor houses in Dorset, with a hall and solar roof dating from the 14th century. Now in the care of English Heritage, it is open to the public in spring and summer (check with Tourist Information for details).

History: In the second half of the 18th century and the early 19th, when smuggling was at its peak, the modest hamlet of Fiddleford was the major smuggling depot of north Dorset. Geographically, it was well placed, being a night's ride from the coast and remote enough to attract little attention from the outside world. In addition, the area had no shortage of people able and willing to boost their income through a little smuggling. As Weymouth's Collector of Customs at Weymouth put it in 1718, the Blackmore Vale of north Dorset was a district "abounding with great numbers of dangerous rogues".

According to local tradition and an article published in 1895, the goods were stored in the farmyard and buildings at Fiddleford Mill and Manor. Successive occupants of the Manor "were requested always to keep the barton and stalls well supplied with hay and straw and not to remove it until all was safe". Here the goods would be left until they could continue their journey later.

The leader of the local gang for many years was Roger Ridout, a miller from Okeford Fitzpaine. A maternal ancestor of co-author Roger Guttridge, Ridout was born a few miles away at Farrington, near Shroton, in 1736, but his connections with Fiddleford were strong. His mother, Susannah (nee Appowell), was a Fiddleford girl and in 1746, at the age of 10, the young Roger inherited the lease on his late grandfather Thomas Appowell's house in the village. In 1756 he married Mary Hancock, of Sturminster Newton, who was later to bear him seven sons.

Roger Ridout is the stuff of legend as well as fact. One story tells how he was challenged by an Excise officer concerning the contents of a jar he was carrying home from Fiddleford Brewery. The smuggler invited him to smell it and the officer agreed. But the jar contained not some dutiable liquor but quick-acting yeast or 'barm' which, when the cork was extracted, sprayed into the officer's eyes, enabling the smuggler to push him into the ditch.

Ridout is also said to have bribed his way out of trouble by leaving tubs of brandy on the doorstep of a Sturminster Newton JP, Mr Dashwood; to have escaped the clutches of the law by climbing down knotted sheets from his bedroom window; to have eventually served time in Dorchester Jail, where he was visited by his wife, who would smuggle in a pig's bladder of ale so her husband could enjoy a secret drink through the bars.

Documentary evidence tends to bear out the legends. The records of Poole Custom House record in 1770 that "Isaac Gulliver, William Beale and Roger Ridout run great quantities of goods on our North shore [the beach at Bournemouth and Sandbanks]". Prisoners tried at the Dorset Assizes in 1781 included Roger, Mary and son William Ridout and Richard Pope, all accused of murdering Thomas Penny but all found not guilty. Prisoners arriving at Dorchester Jail in 1787 included Roger Ridout, miller, of Okeford Fitzpaine, who was released two weeks later after paying a £40 fine for smuggling.

The article published in 1895 names not only Roger Ridout but his horse — Ridout's Stumpted Tail (though Jim Ridout always insisted it was Ridout's Ratted Tail). The Victorian writer states that, late one night in about 1794, his grandfather and father saw the string of smugglers' horses, loaded with contraband, on the narrow road between Okeford Fitzpaine and Fiddleford.

The writer goes on: "One or two men, armed, generally were in front and then 10 or 12 horses connected by ropes or halters followed at a hard trot, and two or three men brought up the rear. This cavalcade did not stop for any person, and it was very difficult to get out of their way, as the roads, until the turnpikes were made in 1824, would only allow of one carriage, except in certain parts. The contraband goods were principally brought from Lulworth and the coast through Whiteparish and Okeford Fitzpaine, through the paths in the woods to Fiddleford, and thus distributed."

Interestingly, the author of this 1895 article was H.C. Dashwood — grandson of Dashwood the magistrate who is supposed to have found tubs of brandy on his doorstep. Perhaps his sighting of the Ridout gang at work, as described by grandson H.C. a century later, is the reason why Roger Ridout felt the need to buy (or reward) his co-operation.

Roger Ridout died in 1811, Mary in 1809, but the smuggling and related activities continued long after their deaths. Three other Okeford Fitzpaine smugglers appear in the Dorchester Prison registers between 1813 and 1825, including Joseph Ridout, a grandson of Roger and Mary, who spent a year in jail after failing to pay a £100 smuggling fine. A certain "Ducky" Pope was a later-leader of the Okeford-Fiddleford gang.

Another smuggling story from Sturminster, which pre-dates the Ridout gang by many years, comes from the report of Treasury investigator William Culliford, whose inquiries led to the suspension of 38 West Country Customs men in 1682. In his report, Culliford describes how the corrupt Surveyor of Customs at Poole, Thomas Barney, visited Sturminster in 1681 with two of his men, John Penny, and tidewaiter Thomas Keeping. They seized five packs of cloth from a Mr Stephens, whose response was to treat Barney and Penny to drinks! According to Keeping, it was four hours before they emerged, by which time Barney was "very much fuddled". While the cloth was loaded on to the horses, the surveyor caused a disturbance among the inhabitants of Sturminster by abusing and striking some women who were looking on. "He made such a riot," said Keeping, "that the people fell upon us and carried away the cloth." In the tidewaiter's opinion, the disturbance had been deliberately provoked by his superior officers "that the goods might be taken from them".

The Walk: On leaving the pub car park, turn right on to the lane. After about 50 yards, fork left on to the footpath (indicated by a wooden footpath marker) and walk along the narrow track, known to locals as Front Lane (the metalled road you have just left is Back Lane!).

The path follows the bank of the Darknoll Brook on the left. On the right are cottages and gardens and you will also pass the back of a mushroom farm.

On rejoining Back Lane, turn left and follow the road over a small bridge until you reach a small group of buildings clustered around a yard. Fiddleford Manor is on the left, the disused mill straight ahead. It was in the old farm buildings in this part of the village that the Ridout gang used to store their contraband a couple of centuries ago.

Walk towards the old mill and as you pass between the buildings, notice the stone equivalent of a welcome mat inscribed on the wall on the right. It is dated 1566 and tells us: "He thatt wyll have here any thynge don / Let him com fryndly he shal be welcom."

The path bears left and bridges a weir, then passes through a narrow tree-lined section before crossing a particularly narrow bridge over a second weir, or rolling bay.

At the end of this bridge is a wooden signpost and a gate. Walk in the direction of Sturminster Newton — the path goes straight across the grass to another footbridge.

After crossing this bridge, follow the sign to Sturminster Newton. The track leads diagonally to the right, across the grass and away from the River Stour.

The path is well trodden and easy to follow as it crosses the large open field. On the hillside beyond the river is the intriguingly-named Piddles Wood, which is particularly attractive in autumn.

The path comes close to the hedge on the right of the field. A little way on, look out for a stile and gate on the same side.

Climb the stile, which is marked with a yellow arrow, and follow the track across the grass. The market town of Sturminster Newton can now be seen straight ahead.

At the end of the field, cross the stile beside the gate and follow the sign to Penny Street.

The path runs between hedges. At the end, turn right into Penny Street, one of Sturminster's older streets, with a varied and interesting selection of houses and cottages. In the 18th and 19th centuries the bottom part of Penny Street — known as Gotts Corner and Tanyard — produced much of the special wool-based cloth known as "swanskin" for the crews of the cod ships which sailed each spring from Poole to Newfoundland.

Some way up Penny Street on the right is the elegant Vine House. Around 1800 this was the home of Mr Dashwood, the magistrate allegedly bribed by Roger Ridout. Was it on this doorstep that the smuggler left tubs of brandy to buy the owner's silence?

Follow Penny Street to the top and bear right into the Market Place, which has been the hub of this very old riverside town for many centuries. The sprinkling of shops, pubs and cafes may tempt you to linger awhile before continuing the walk.

When you are ready to continue, turn right into Station Road (a few yards beyond the Swan Hotel on the right).

After walking a short distance, turn right towards Barnes Close, then left into the car park.

At the far end take the footpath signposted Fiddleford Manor and Mill.

The weir at Fiddleford Mill

Follow the path, which runs along the old Somerset and Dorset railway line, closed by the Beeching cuts in the 1960s. The stone chippings which once formed the bed of the track can still be seen.

The path runs between blackberry bushes on an embankment over the water meadows, then across farmland.

On reaching the remains of the railway bridge which formerly spanned the river, go down the steps and turn right, over the stile.

The path runs alongside the river, towards Fiddleford Mill which is visible in the distance.

On approaching the mill pond, cross a small bridge, and then follow the track across the grass to turn left on to the bridges crossed on the outward journey.

Retrace your steps to the Fiddleford Inn.

TALES OF SQUIRES AND SMUGGLERS
Kingston and Encombe

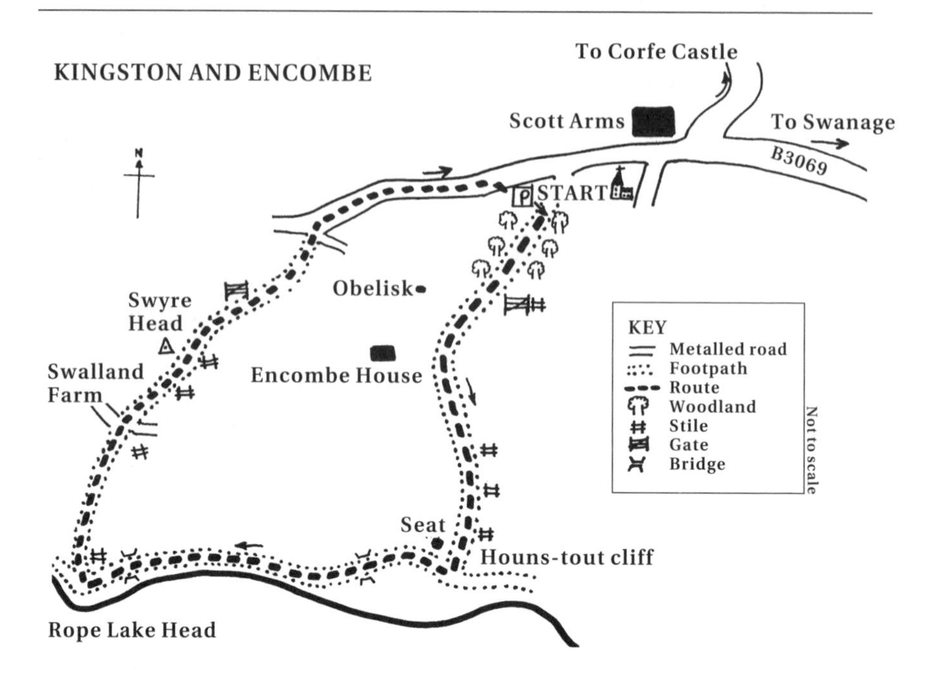

Distance: 8 kms (5 miles).

Maps: OS Landranger 195 Bournemouth, Purbeck and surrounding area. Map Ref: SY 953 795.
OS Outdoor Leisure 15 Purbeck.

Degree of difficulty: This walk is recommended for its exceptional views but is best walked in dry conditions, as there are one or two steep, grassy descents on the cliff path. Unfenced stretches near the clifftop make it unsuitable for young children. There is a very steep path to the top of Swyre Head.

How to get there: From Wareham, take the A351 through Corfe Castle. As you leave the village by the Swanage road, turn right on to the B3069 to Kingston. Follow the signs to the car park.

Parking: There is free parking at the western edge of Kingston (signposted). The Scott Arms has an ample car park for patrons.

Pub facilities: The Scott Arms at Kingston is a charming old world Greenalls pub with a coat of Virginia creeper outside and inside a veritable rabbit warren of bar rooms and other nooks and crannies on several levels. One bar and the large beer garden offer superb views of Corfe Castle and beyond. The walls and large fireplaces sport a variety of old pictures, farm implements and other historic objects.

The Scott Arms, Kingston

The pub was built in the 18th century as part of the Encombe estate and was originally known as the Eldon Arms after Lord Eldon, a Lord Chancellor of England, who owned the estate. A curiosity in the garden is the authentic-looking gravestone of "Michael Henchard, 1807-1852, formerly Mayor of Casterbridge" — a memento left by film-makers who were in the village to shoot a film based on the Thomas Hardy novel.

The menu includes light lunchtime snacks and more substantial "quarryman's dinners" at lunchtimes and in the evenings. There is also a daily selection of specials and some elabroate ice cream desserts, not to mention a a good selection of wines, beers and real ales. The pub is popular with walkers and cyclists. Children are welcome except in the Quarr Bar, described as a "sanctuary for adults"!

Opening times: 11 am-2.30 pm and 6-11 pm Monday-Saturday, 12 noon-3 pm and 7-10.30 pm Sunday. Tel: 01929 480270.

History: Two centuries ago the village of Kingston was a hotbed of smuggling but a few decades earlier the same area produced one of the nation's most successful investigators of the contraband trade. William Culliford was the son of Robert Culliford, owner of Encombe Manor and MP for Wareham. In later life he entered Parliament himself as the member for Corfe Castle and was also Commissioner of Customs for Scotland and Ireland. But as a young man he worked for the Treasury and was entrusted in 1681 with the task of investigating frauds, corruption and smuggling in South Wales and South West England. He was a particularly diligent detective and his inquiries led to the suspension of no less than 38 Customs officers, including several at the Dorset ports of Poole, Weymouth and Lyme Regis. At Weymouth Culliford described the Collector of Customs himself, Mr

The 'memorial' to the fictitious Mayor of Casterbridge Michael Henchard

Miller, as "a person of debauched life and conversation, who seldom goes to bed till three or four o'clock in the morning and many times not all night"!

The Cullifords owned Encombe Manor until 1734, when it was bought by John Pitt, a cousin of the statesman William Pitt, Earl of Chatham. The present house – which can be seen from certain points on the walk – dates from John Pitt's time. In fact, it was partly designed by him, as he was a squire with architectural aspirations. A philanthropic descendant of John Pitt, William Morton Pitt, had other ambitions, one of which was to lure the local population away from smuggling. In order to "detach them from the pursuit of that illicit traffic which, from the contiguous situation of this place to the sea coast, they had long been able to follow", William Morton Pitt opened a factory for making rope, twine, sackcloth, dowlas and sailcloth. The factory – opened in the 1770s – created 200 jobs and was described by the 18th century Dorset historian the Rev John Hutchins as "a noble example to those who are blessed by Providence with the means of providing for the wants and necessities of their fellow creatures". Sadly, the fellow creatures were less than appreciative. A later edition of Hutchins records: "The manufactory established by Mr Pitt, having proved unsuccessful, was soon abandoned."

Popular landing places for contraband in these parts included Winspit, where a rare break in the cliffs enabled smugglers to take horses to the shore, and Chapman's Pool, a secluded cove between the high cliffs of Houns-tout and St Alban's (or Aldhelm's) Head. A story is told of one landing at Chapman's Pool which threatened to end in disaster when the approaching boat was spotted by a coastguard. The officer in question, whose name was Pat, was feeling particularly zealous following a briefing in which he and his colleagues had been urged to put a stop to smuggling on this part of the coast. From his hiding place near the shore, he shouted three times, "Who comes here?", then fired his musket over the smugglers' heads. Remembering that one of their friends had recently been shot in similar circumstances, the smugglers decided to come quietly rather than flee. But instead of arresting them, Pat shouted that he could not allow them to land their goods. "I have strict orders not to allow any smuggling along our coast," he said. "So be off with you at once." The smugglers could hardly believe their luck and

Drystone walls are a common feature of the landscape around Kingston and Corfe Castle

wasted no time in obeying the instructions. Pat was also rather pleased with himself. Next day he smugly told the chief coastguard how he had thwarted a run of contraband and hinted that it might lead to a stripe across his arm. "You brainless loon! If I recommend you for anything, it'll be stripes across your back," the senior officer replied.

During another landing at Chapman's Pool, one of the smugglers fell in a ditch and broke his leg. He was carried to his home at Kingston and one of his chums set off for Swanage with two horses. Just before midnight a certain Swanage doctor answered the door and found a masked man on the doorstep. After some discussion, the doctor agreed to accompany his visitor on an errand of mercy. He even allowed the man to put a sack over his head. Then he mounted the spare horse, which was turned around three or four times before being led away at a fast trot. There was no hold-up at the Swanage turnpike, as the keeper had earlier been bribed to leave the gate open all night. When the two horsemen finally reached their destination, the doctor was led into a cottage and the sack removed from his head. He found himself in a room with seven or eight strong men, all masked, and his patient, also masked. He did his work, received his fee, accepted the sack over his head again and was led back to Swanage – unaware of where he had been or who he had treated and unable to give any meaningful evidence against the patient or his companions.

The Walk: From the car park take the gravel path signposted to Houns-tout. This easy stretch leads through woodland scented with wild garlic and bluebells in spring.

After leaving the trees behind, the path climbs gently. At the top of the hill you can stop at the gate to admire the view to Swyre Head and the sea.

Climb over the stile and continue walking, keeping the dry stone wall on your left. In the deep valley to your right you will have a bird's eye view of Encombe House, childhood home of the 17th century investigator William Culliford. An obelisk visible on the far side of the valley was erected in 1835 by the then owner of Encombe, Lord Eldon, in memory of his brother, Lord Stowell.

Once you have climbed the wooden stile, the distant Isle of Portland comes into view. After two more stiles you will find yourself on a very exposed headland where a west-facing seat of Purbeck stone offers a stunning vista over the cliffs to Tyneham, Lulworth and beyond. Landmarks include Clavel's Tower, Kimmeridge, in the middle distance.

From the seat head west towards the view you have just been admiring and walk down the steep grassy path beside the wire fence. With luck you may see buzzards wheeling overhead. To the left is evidence of recent cliff falls. The path leads between some bushes and emerges on to a short slippery descent to a bridge over a ducted stream, which ends in a waterfall over the edge of the cliff.

Climb the next slope and look back to see just how far you have walked. The stone seat is just a speck on the clifftop.

The next part of the walk is over undulating clifftop. The path is bumpy and close to the edge – and there is no fence, so please take care!

After crossing a stream by way of two sturdy planks, look out for a milestone at Rope Lake Head pointing to Swyre Head three quarters of a mile away. Climb the adjacent stile and head inland, keeping to the edge of the field.

At the northern end of the path, climb the wooden stile and walk straight on, along the Swallow Farm track. At the end of the track, climb the wooden stile and look up to see another directly above, at the top of Swyre.

The path goes straight up and its steepness will tax the leg muscles of all but the fittest walkers. But at the summit your efforts will be reward by by one of the finest views in the Isle of Purbeck. From this vantage point more than 600 feet (200 metres) above sea level, you can see a stunning panorama. The coastline stretches away towards Portland and the oil tankers loading at Kimmeridge look like toys. In the other direction lie Poole Harbour and Brownsea Island, Poole Bay, Bournemouth and the Isle of Wight.

A stone sign will direct you down the hill towards the car park and Kingston. As you walk along the ridge you will be able to look down on Encombe House from the other side.

When you arrive at a small gate, follow the blue arrow which points diagonally across the field. Pass the sheep pens, walk between the pillars and turn right on to the metalled road. This leads straight back to the car park and gives an unusual north-south view of Corfe Castle.

GULLIVER'S HEATH
West Moors and Holt Heath

Distance: 3 kms (1.9 miles)

Maps: OS Landranger 195 Bournemouth, Purbeck and surrounding area. Map Ref: SZ 079 031.

Degree of difficulty: This walk is easy, and the ideal choice if you are looking for a short stroll on level ground. There may be one or two muddy patches.

How to get there: From the A31 Ferndown bypass, follow the signs to West Moors. The Tap and Railway is in Station Road, part of the B3072 which runs through the centre of the village.

Parking: Patrons of the Tap and Railway may use the pub's spacious car park providing they intend to use the pub. There is also a large public car park within easy walking distance.

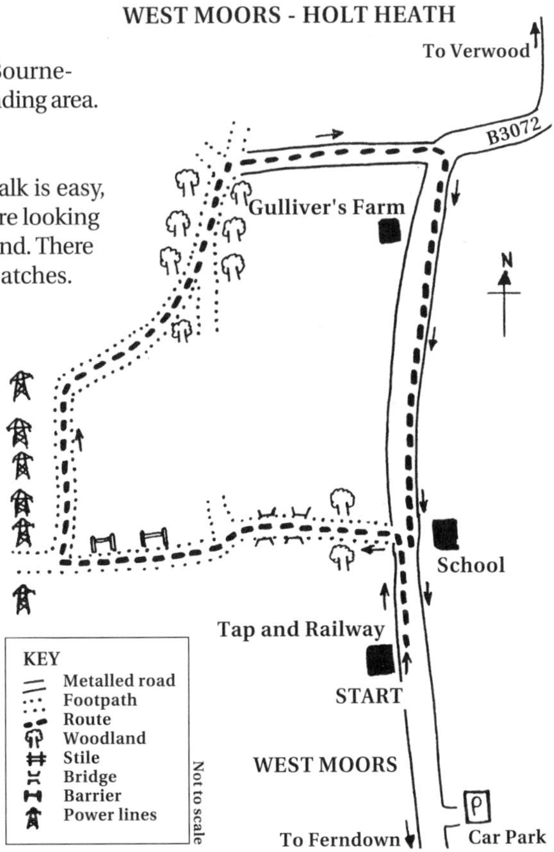

Pub facilities: The Tap and Railway is a sizeable family pub in Station Road, West Moors. Food is served throughout the day and evening. The menu is comprehensive, ranging from sandwiches and burgers to a full steak meal. There is also a "hungry man" menu with a certificate awarded to anyone successfuly tackling the enormous meal! A range of real ales is also available. Facilities include a well-equipped family room and a large beer garden with picnic tables and children's play equipment.

Opening times: 11 am-11 pm Monday-Saturday, 12 noon-10.30 pm Sunday. Tel: 01202 897166.

History: West Moors today has a population of 7,000 but less than 200 years

The Tap and Railway, West Moors

ago it comprised a mere handful of isolated farms scattered across the heath. In fact, the area was still sparsely populated when it suddenly found itself in the railway age in 1867. Because of its geographical position, it was honoured with its own railway station and even a junction, though initially it drew most of its passengers from the larger (though by no means large) village of Ferndown to the south.

Looking at the first Ordnance Survey map of the area, published in 1811, it is not hard to see why this was good smuggling country. From the smuggling communities of Kinson, Longham and Christchurch, from the deserted beaches between Sandbanks and Hengistbury Head, tracks led across the wild commons and heaths towards the New Forest and Cranborne Chase, where smugglers could quickly disappear with their contraband. The clues are all around. Smugglers Cottage in Wimborne Road, Tricketts Cross, a short distance from West Moors, dates from the great smuggling age and was almost certainly used by contraband traders who made their way across the heath. It was badly damaged by fire in recent years but has been restored in the original style. Nearby, the Smugglers Haunt pub provides another reminder of smuggling days. The pub itself post-dates the smuggling age but until the early years of the 20th century, a much older building stood in the grounds.

But the strongest link with smuggling days is at West Moors itself, where an old farmhouse helps to keep alive the name of the most successful freetrader in Dorset history. Gulliver's Farm faces the B3072 road through the village and features in the walk. A couple of centuries ago it belonged to Isaac Gulliver, one of many rural properties which pro-

Gulliver's Farm and (left of picture) the 18th century barn, said to be the oldest building at West Moors

vided him with labourers, horses and wagons to move his contraband, and barns and outhouses in which to hide goods under hay and straw.

Gulliver was the greatest smuggler in these parts and the most famous. Even his arch opponent, the Collector of Customs at Poole, once described him in an official report to London as "a man of great speculating genius". His beginnings in Wiltshire were humble and working class but he was very much a man of his time and he rose, through smuggling, to a position of great wealth and social respectability. His smuggling empire was vast, covering the whole of Dorset and extending beyond Lyme Regis in the south-west, northwards into Wiltshire and eastwards into Hampshire and the New Forest.

Isaac Gulliver survived into his late seventies, dying in 1822 in his retirement home in West Borough, Wimborne, which is still called Gulliver's House. He left an estate worth £60,000, including property spread over four counties, and was buried within the walls of Wimborne Minster, where he had served as a churchwarden in later life. A memorial stone, its simple inscription worn away by generations of Wimborne feet, hangs under the west tower.

The Walk: Turn left out of the pub car park and walk along the pavement until you come to a footpath on the left, opposite St Mary's First School. It is signposted Fryers Fields Walk.

Follow the path between a wire fence and some bushes. There is a sports field on the right.

Walk straight on, ignoring the path to the right. Go through the trees and over two sturdy wooden bridges, both

Isaac Gulliver

Elizabeth Gulliver

marked with a yellow arrow, and continue along the gravel track.

The path opens out on to heathland and passes beneath power lines.

At a house called Lynmoor, bear right, ignoring the stile with the yellow arrow. Pass the wooden barrier and you will see a Holt nature reserve sign on the right.

After the second barrier the track runs out and becomes a narrow path.

At the next set of overhead cables follow the blue arrow pointing to the right. The path leads across the heath, which is full of interesting plant and animal life, including dragonflies and several types of heather. You may even see a fox.

The open track follows the line of power cables. Counting the pylons by the path as "1", when you reach the fifth set look out for a blue arrow low down on the right, where the path turns to the right.

Follow the blue arrows into the birch trees and at the end of this path turn left on to a gravel road, which is Newman's Lane.

Bear right at the corner and carry on past the smallholdings to the end of the road.

Turn right on to the B3072 Station Road, the main road through the village. There is a pavement on the left.

On the right is Gulliver's Farm, an attractive house with an interesting circular window on the first floor. It takes its name from its association with the smuggler Isaac Gulliver (see History section).

Follow Station Road back to the Tap and Railway .

Walk No: 8

BRANDY ON THE ROCK
Portland and the Bill

Distance: 6.4 kms (4 miles)

Maps: OS Landranger 194 Dorchester, Weymouth and surrounding area.
Map ref: SY 678 687.

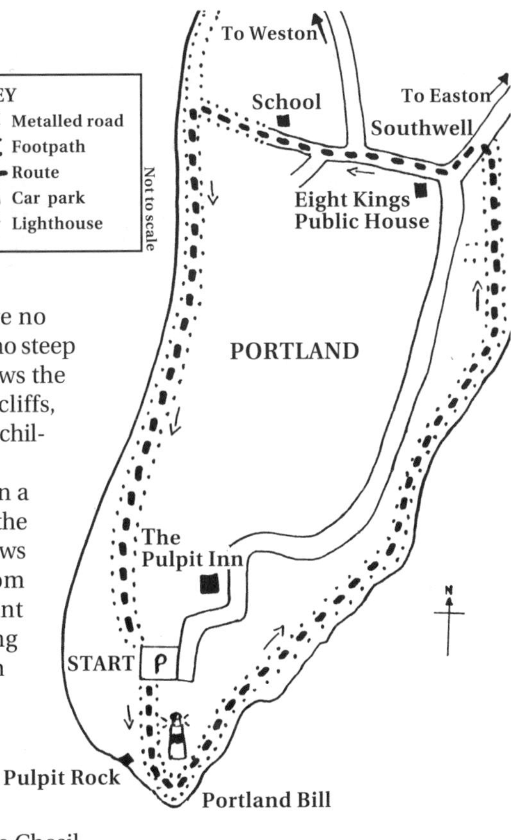

Degree of difficulty: There are no gates or stiles on this walk and no steep climbs. Most of the route follows the coastal path along unfenced cliffs, making it unsuitable for young children.

It is also a walk to be done on a clear day to take advantage of the sweeping views. The walk follows the eastern coastal path, from which can be seen the distant Purbeck Hills, before turning inland through a village to return along the western coastal path.

How to get there: From Weymouth follow the A354 through Wyke Regis and along the causeway (part of the Chesil Bank) which connects the Isle of Portland to the mainland. Once on Portland, follow the signs to Easton and the Bill.

Parking: There is a large pay and display car park near the lighthouse, a short distance from the Pulpit Inn. The pub itself has a sizable car park for patrons; walkers intending to use the pub may also park there *by prior arrangement with the landlord.*

Pub facilities: The Pulpit Inn is a large Gibbs Mew pub built in the 1950s near the most southerly tip of Portland, and of Dorset. It is just a few yards from Portland Bill and the Pulpit Rock and has an almost panoramic view of the sea. It has a restaurant and offers a wide selection of snacks and meals including homemade pizza and many vegetarian choices. Customers are asked to be patient while waiting for their order, as most of the food is freshly prepared. The terrace

The Pulpit Inn, Portland Bill

shares the sea views. There is also a children's area and accommodation is available. Opening times: 11.30 am-3 pm and 6.30-11 pm Monday-Saturday, 12 noon-4 pm and 7-11 pm Sunday. Tel: 01305 821237.

Optional extras: Binoculars or a telescope will help to make the most of the dramatic views over land and sea and, for birdwatchers, the wide range of species to be seen here, especially in the migration season. For vast numbers of birds each spring, Portland provides the first opportunity to rest and feed after the long flight across the sea.

Other attractions: Portland Bill Lighthouse is often open to visitors. For those game enough to climb the 153 steps to the top, there are magnificent views over coast and sea, plus the chance to take a close look at the lamp, capable of projecting its beam of light to a distance of 18 miles on a clear night.

History: As you trudge along Portland's rugged clifftops, admiring the views of sea and coast and watching the great tankers and container ships ploughing the shipping lanes, it is not hard to imagine the days when all ships were powered by sail or oar. With the help of the Weymouth Custom House records, it is even less difficult to push the mind back one further step to the great smuggling age. One report in particular, sent from Weymouth to the Customs headquarters in London in 1738, paints a vivid picture of the contraband operations. It describes how the smugglers collected their goods from the Channel Islands of Guernsey or Alderney, where they waited for "a favourable but pretty stiff gale of wind" before leaving for England.

The report continues: "On making the Isle of Portland, or St Alban's Head, they bring to, lay a-hull or are under an easy

View from Portland Bill showing a crane used in the stone industry

sail until night, when they make for the first convenient place along shore, and there they sink their brandy and immediately carry off their tea in their boat, and land the same, lodging among the rocks, bushes, ditches and fields adjoining, where it can be most conveniently secured until it can be carried off, which is generally the same night or the next after."

Two or three hundred years ago those whose business it was to be on Portland's clifftops would from time to time find themselves witnessing incidents between smugglers and revenue officials. One such incident occurred in 1718, at the very dawn of the great smuggling age. It followed an attempt by a Weymouth Customs team, led by tide surveyor John Cook, to board a pair of smuggling boats in the sheltered anchorage known as Portland Roads. Soon the officers were fighting for their lives. As Weymouth's Collector of Customs reported, "The both boats got together, and having each seven or eight lusty Portland fellows, they not only kept him [Cook] from boarding them but beat and wounded them at a most unmerciful rate, and particularly one John Morris of this town, a hired man, who exerted himself very extraordinarily in assisting the officers, and had his right arm broken in two places, besides other wounds, and now lies in danger of his life thereby."

On the morning of April 10, 1734, Portlanders watched another drama unfold. It began at 5 am when Captain James Stears and the crew of the Walker revenue sloop spotted a smuggling vessel, the Speedwell, three or four miles off Portland Bill. They tried to approach but there was little wind and after four hours the Walker had made little progress. At 9 o'clock Captain Stears ordered his chief mate and six hands to take up the chase in a rowing boat. No sooner had they put off from the mother vessel than the smugglers turned their ship and stood to sea. The chase continued for a further five hours and it was 2 pm before the rowing boat finally came alongside the Speedwell nine nautical miles from where it had started. But catching the ship was one thing; boarding her was quite another. Twice the revenue men tried to scramble on to the Speedwell; twice they were repulsed by smugglers armed with handspikes and pieces of a broken flagpole, causing injuries to two of them.

At the third attempt the Speedwell was successfully boarded, its cargo revealed and its crew identified. The skipper was Richard Morris, a man "wholly employed in the smuggling trade". His crew were all notorious smugglers and there also four passengers, all of whom had shares in the cargo. The goods consisted of 68 casks of brandy, rum and wine, 14 bags of tea and six cakes of soap. From one of the crew, Giles Sergent, who agreed to cooperate with officials, probably in exchange for immunity from prosecution, they learned that the Speedwell had sailed from Weymouth on March 30, collected her cargo from Guernsey and begun the return voyage on April 6. Their plan had been to run the goods on "any convenient place" on the Dorset coast, preferably Portland or West Lulworth.

On Portland itself, the minds and backgrounds of the inhabitants had equipped them well for the active part they were destined to play in the smuggling trade. Although Portland is not a true island (it is connected to the mainland by the Chesil Beach), its relative isolation in the past produced an island mentality among its native people. "The Portlanders not only kept to themselves, but were exceedingly jealous of strangers; they married only with their own folk, and possessed curious laws and still more curious morals," wrote Sir Frederick Treves in 1906.

Quarrying was Portland's traditional industry and its rocky landscape still bears the scars. Portlanders made good use of their greatest resource, as Henry VIII's topographer John Leland noted in 1540: "The people be good there in flinging of stones, and use it for the defence of the isle." Wrecking was another traditional occupation hereabouts with almost every major storm bringing an unfortunate vessel on to the rocks or Chesil Beach for the locals to plunder.

When large scale smuggling arrived on the scene, it was inevitable that this relatively lawless community of stone-slinging wreckers would wholeheartedly embrace it. They did, sometimes with help from those whose job it was to prevent them. In 1681, a Customs raiding party from Weymouth seized a parcel of contraband from a room where their Portland colleague John Peters "was the same time drinking".

Official records from the 18th and 19th centuries hint repeatedly at the remarkable extent of Portland's involvement in smuggling and the arrogance of the smugglers. In 1740 Customs officers wrote of "the whole scene of that scandalous trade in Portland" and their hope (probably a vain hope) that a certain informer was about to expose it. A few years later, Customs men were reluctant to visit Portland at all "for fear of being knocked in the head by a volley of stones".

Many other incidents are chronicled, as in 1747, when a mob more than 20 strong stoned the crew of a revenue sloop as they searched boats near Portland Castle. In 1762, 150 Portlanders fought with Customs officers over casks of brandy washed ashore from a Cornish smuggling vessel wrecked in a storm with the loss of all crew. In 1767, after another Portland affray, an Excise officer faced prosecution for shooting a smuggler in the leg. And in 1784, an officer from the *Alarm* revenue lugger was hit with an oar during a confrontation in Chesil Cove. A crowd of Portlanders then "armed themselves with bludgeons" and forced the *Alarm* to withdraw. "We could not do more in executing our duty without the utmost threat to our lives," reported the *Alarm's* commander.

Three years after this incident, the crews of two revenue cutters had to contend with a mob of 200 Portlanders as they tried to seize a raft of tubs from the sea. Two officers were "struck, abused and very ill-treated"; others were stoned. Several Portlanders ended up at the Dorset Assizes but the judge ruled in their favour on the grounds that they were merely trying to prevent the officers taking a boat which was their rightful property. The ruling had far-reaching implications for the local Customs men.

The arrogance of the Portlanders is demonstrated by an incident which occurred in 1822. It involved a race between smugglers and Customs officers to reach a raft of brandy tubs which had earlier been sunk in the sea but had now been broken up by a storm and floated to the surface. The Customs men set off first but the smugglers hoisted a sail and overtook them, the man at the helm "striking his posterior in derision" as they passed! With the aid of additional stones, the smugglers succeeded

The lamp in Portland lighthouse

in re-sinking the raft but the officers eventually managed to bring them to the surface again and seized 28 tubs.

Nothing provides more comprehensive evidence of Portland's involvement in smuggling than the registers of Dorchester Prison. Between 1817 and 1845 no less than 129 Portlanders are listed for smuggling-related offences, more than from any other Dorset community. Smuggling continued in Portland until at least 1849, the year when the harbour breakwater built by Portland prisoners was opened. According to the old Dorset smuggling historian W.M. Hardy, smugglers took advantage of the absence of coastguards for the opening by Prince Albert to land a cargo and lodge it in a pub called Sampsons.

The Walk: On leaving the car park, walk the short distance to Portland Bill Lighthouse, with its distinctive red horizontal stripe. It is 136 feet high and was built in 1905 to replace the Lower Lighthouse, which is now a bird observatory and field centre. If the working lighthouse is open, you have the option to tread the 153 steps to the top before continuing your walk.

On leaving the lighthouse, stand on the viewing area at the cliff edge and observe the Pulpit Rock to your right. This natural feature was originally an arch called White Hole; but in 1875 part of it was removed by quarry workers, leaving a stack.

Follow the track across the grass to the path which runs north, along the eastern coast.

Offshore, there are vicious currents and roaring waves. This walk was done in a force eight gale, with the sea boiling and crashing against the rocks. In such conditions it is not hard to see how Portland earned its reputation as a graveyard for shipping in the past. Even the lifeboat was having difficulty rounding the Bill, seeming to stop from time to time on the crest of a wave before plunging out of view behind the rollers.

There are a few derricks at the edge of the low cliff, used for lowering blocks of stone on to ships.

Walk between the beach huts and follow the track. This area is cross-crossed with footpaths, but ours lies straight ahead. So many other walks in this book feature Portland as a dark wedge on a distant horizon. From the wedge itself, it is interesting to look across the sea to Osmington Mills, Lulworth Cove, Houns Tout and all the way to St Aldhelm's (or Alban's) Head.

After a short distance the chimneys of the Verne Prison come into view on the horizon, and the path goes through disused quarries, where blocks of stone are precariously piled and the seams of rock can be easily seen in the cliff.

Follow the path, which runs near the cliff edge.

At the stone waymarker, walk straight on, along the coast path. The track leads uphill and comes out on to the main road.

Turn left, and walk into the village of Southwell — there is a pavement all the way.

Stay on this road, which bears right by the Eight Kings pub.

Take the next road on the left, Sweet Hill Road, and then Sweet Hill Lane, which is a cul-de-sac.

Pass the children's playground, and the bungalows. At Southwell Primary School the road ends. Walk straight on, along the open track, keeping the Ministry of Defence establishment on your left.

At the end of the track, turn left on to the cliff path, where a stunning panoramic view of Lyme Bay opens up.

The sweep of the Chesil Beach, with Weymouth to the right, leads the eye past the Fleet to Golden Cap, Lyme Regis and the coast of south Devon.

The cliffs on this side of Portland are much higher than those on the east and the sea can be seen swirling on to the rocks below. On a stormy day it is easy to see how gigantic waves sometimes go right over the Chesil Bank.

The path leads past Old Higher Lighthouse, across the grass and downhill to the Pulpit Inn and Portland Bill.

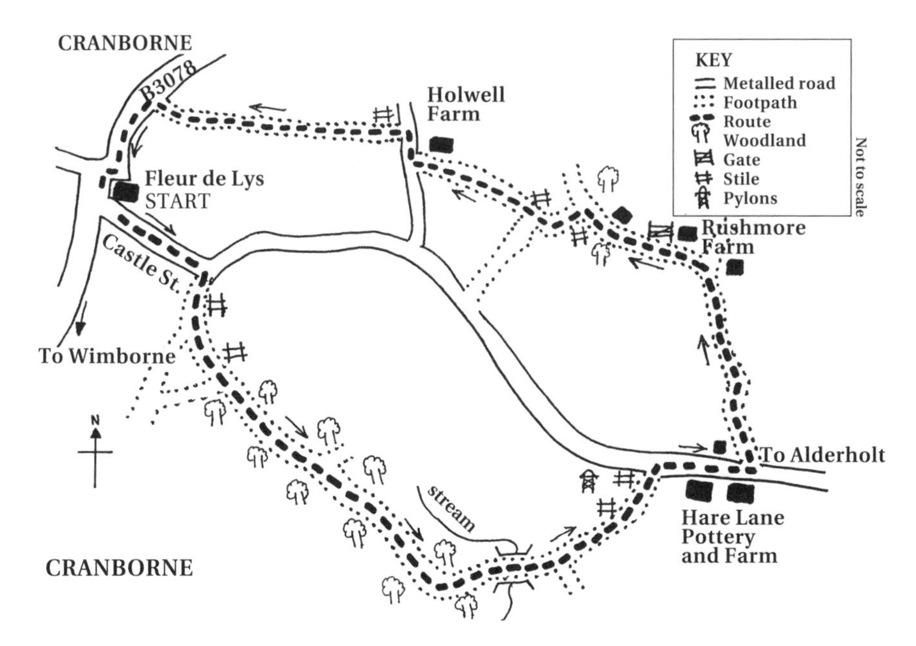

Distance: 7 kms (4.4 miles)

Maps: OS Landranger 195 Bournemouth, Purbeck and surrounding area. Map ref: SU 056 134.

Degree of difficulty: Apart from a few stiles and two hills, this is an easy walk, although one stretch will be muddy in all but the driest weather as it runs alongside a stream. Most of the walk is in the shelter of woodland, which makes it a good choice for a windy day.

How to get there: From Wimborne, follow the B3078 to Cranborne, looking out for the Fleur de Lys on the right as you approach the village centre.

Parking: Walkers intending to use the Fleur de Lys are invited to use the pub car park providing they speak to the landlord beforehand. Parking is also available in side streets.

Pub facilities: The Fleur de Lys, a Hall and Woodhouse pub, has been quenching the thirst of customers for at least 300 years, while the building itself has Norman origins. Not surprisingly, it boasts a genuine olde worlde atmosphere and it is not hard to imagine the days when smugglers would huddle around the open fire discussing their past and future ventures. There is still a log fire in winter.

Notable former customers of the Fleur de Lys include not only the Verwood smuggler Dan Sims (see History section)

The Fleur de Lys, Cranborne

but Judge Jeffreys of Bloody Assize fame, the poet Rupert Brooke, who wrote a poem here, and Thomas Hardy, whose character Tess of the D'Urbervilles used to dance in a barn behind the pub before walking home to Trentridge (Pentridge).

The pub serves breakfasts from 8 am as well as morning coffee, lunches and evening meals. The breakfasts are popular with customers who like to eat there before setting out for a morning walk. The extensive menu includes snacks, "small bites", grills, vegetarian dishes and lots of specials as well as a small selection of bar snacks in the Village Bar. Traditional ales are also available, as is overnight accommodation in eight ensuite double or twin rooms. There is also a beer garden.

Opening times: Breakfasts from 8 am; licensed opening 10.30 am-2.30 pm (and sometimes all afternoon), 6-11 pm Monday-Saturday, 12 noon-3 pm and 7-10.30 pm Sunday. Tel 01725 517282.

Optional extras: Good boots or wellies are recommended if it has been raining recently.

Other attractions: Cranborne Manor gardens and garden centre. Situated almost opposite the Fleur de Lys. Tel 01725 517248.

The walk also passes **Hare Lane Pottery,** where terracotta pots are made in a wood-fired kiln. Tel 01725 517700.

Attractions in neighbouring villages include the **Heavy Horse Centre,** near Verwood (tel 01202 824040).

History: The Fleur de Lys features in a smuggling story which first appeared in print in 1893 but which probably occurred a century or so earlier. The Victorian account identifies the central character only as "Dan of Verwood" but adds that he died in 1826, at the age of 67, following a fall from his horse. By using this information in conjuction with the Cranborne parish registers, it is possible to identify him as Daniel Sims, who did indeed live at Verwood, which in his time was not the sizeable "new town" of today but a small and scattered hamlet more commonly known as Fairwood (the letter "F" is pronounced "V" by speakers of Dorset dialect). The tale concerns an incident which may well have occurred long before 1826, when Sims was a much younger man.

According to the story, he was cutting turves on Verwood Common when his brother-in-law rode up and informed him that the Excise officer from Cranborne had just carried out a search of his cottage and seized 11 casks of liquor. Sims went straight home for his horse, rode to Cranborne and tied his mount in the stable at the Fleur de Lys. Then he "went into the bar and sat himself quietly down in the chimney corner, with his pipe and glass, as he was wont to do. Soon in comes someone full of the discovery that had been made that morning; Dan quickly ascertained that the kegs were lodged in the Excise man's house, which stood at the corner of the street opposite the present Post Office [ie the Post Office of 1893]."

Armed with this information, Sims finished his pint, left the inn and rode off at a gallop to "concert a plan for the recovery of the spoils with friends of his, desperate characters, who lived somewhere near the coast". Before the day was out several horsemen and a horse and cart (our Victorian source says "carts and horses" in the plural but this seems unlikely for 11 four-and-a-quarter gallon tubs) were on their way to Cranborne, which they reached around midnight. They stopped just outside the village at Deadman's Cross, so called from a legend that a suicide was buried there (the burial of suicides in consecrated ground was forbidden). A local man and close acquatinance of Sims, who was acting as a guide for the smugglers, went on ahead and scrawled a cross in chalk on the door of the Excise man's house. "Being made sure of their prize, the ruffians soon followed, and one of them beat in the door with a sledge-hammer whilst another stood in the street with a loaded horse-pistol, threatening to blow out the Excise man's brains, or of any other person who threatened to resist them. Having secured the goods, they soon loaded their carts and horses, and with one outrider in front, armed, and another in the rear, they galloped away with them."

A short distance from the Fleur de Lys, almost opposite Cranborne Manor, is another house of substance, Cranborne Lodge, which at the beginning of the 19th century was the home of the man known as "the founder of Bournemouth", Captain Lewis Tregonwell. In recent decades one or two writers on smuggling have pointed a finger of suspicion at Tregonwell, though the evidence to support the theory of his involvement is both thin and circumstantial. Coincidentally, however, Cranborne Lodge itself was under suspicion in Tregonwell's own time, though he was only 11 when this occurred. This was in 1769, when the early Georgian mansion was owned by another respectable gentleman, Thomas Erle Drax. A contem-

Pots stacked at the Hare Lane Pottery

porary newspaper report tells us that the house was entered by a Customs officer "under pretence of searching for prohibited goods". Nothing was found and Drax subsequently sued the Customs service and was awarded the then substantial sum of £100 in damages.

The Walk: The Fleur de Lys is situated on the corner of the B3078 and Castle Street. Walk along Castle Street past the houses. Where the road bends sharply to the left, turn into the unnamed gravel road on the right, opposite the Castle Street sign.

A few yards along on the left is a stile with a yellow arrow. Having climbed it, cross the field to the wooden stile which you will see ahead of you diagonally to the left.

Once over this second stile, turn left along the bridleway, following the blue arrow.

The sunken path goes through mixed

woodland (locals may tell you that sunken tracks were often popular with smugglers because of the additional protection they offered from unwanted eyes and ears). Ignore the path which forks to the right.

After about a mile, on reaching the point where the track divides, take the right fork marked with a blue arrow (which may be faded) on a tree. There is a curved bank straight ahead and an unmarked track to the left.

The path goes through light woodland and there is a stream in the wooded area to the left.

The track bears left, crosses a bridge over the stream and goes up a steep incline. At the footpath sign follow the yellow arrow which points to the left and carry on up the slope.

Walk straight on along the path, which winds between tree-topped banks. Where the track opens out and becomes wide and grassy, there are good views over the surrounding woods and farmland.

As you approach Hare Lane Farm there are buildings on the right. The footpath goes straight on over a stile marked with a yellow arrow. It runs parallel to the pylons on the left and there is a garden on the right.

The next stile is on a bank. Be careful, as it takes you rather abruptly on to the Cranborne to Alderholt road.

Turn right on to the road and after a few yards you will come to Hare Lane Pottery, where visitors are welcome.

A little further on, just after the bungalow on the left, is a bridleway on the same side. Turn into it, and walk as far as the cottage on the right.

Turn left on to the track opposite the cottage, marked with a blue arrow on a telegraph pole. It passes Rushmore Farm, a brick and flint building.

At the crest of the rise go through the gate and straight along the wide track, ignoring the path to the left.

When you reach an isolated cottage there are views to the left as far as Bournemouth. The Albany tower block on the East Cliff is visible on a clear day.

Just past the cottage look out for the yellow arrow in the trees on the left and follow it over a stile.

Keeping the fence to your right, follow the track across rough grass.

At the point where the fence turns off at a right angle and the barns of Holwell Farm come into view straight ahead in the distance, head towards them.

The exit from the field is ahead of you at the bottom of the hill in the left-hand or south-west corner, where it meets the track leading to the farm.

At the bottom corner of the field are two stiles and two paths marked with yellow arrows. Take the one which leads towards the barn.

The track is wide and grassy between hedgerows and leads past Holwell Farm, seen earlier from the top of the hill.

Once past the farm buildings walk straight on until you reach a metalled road. Turn right on to it, and then almost immediately left, over a stile marked with a yellow arrow.

Keeping the fence to your left, walk straight up the side of the field, which at the time of writing had been left as a grassy strip.

The track leads down into the village. Once back on tarmac, the route passes a sports field and houses. At the main road, turn left and follow it back to the Fleur de Lys.

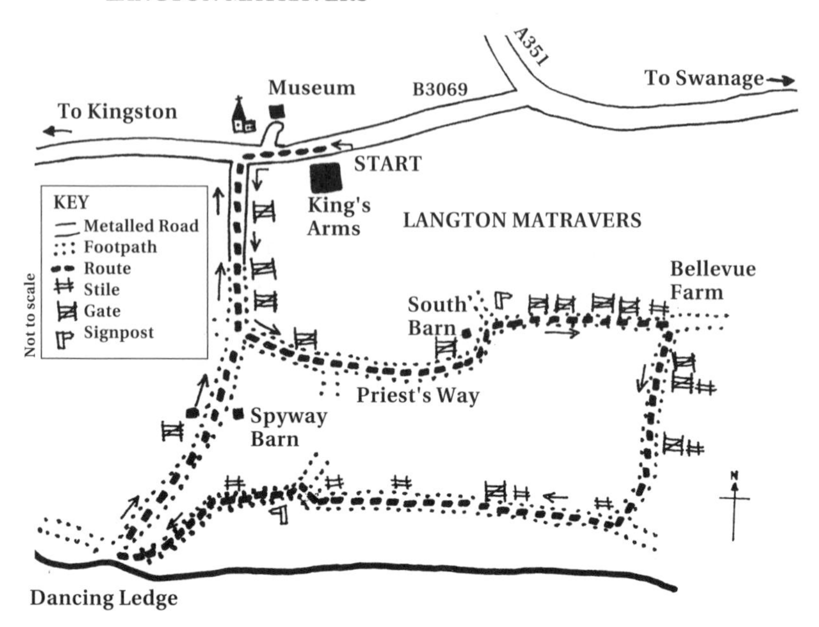

Distance: Approx 8 kms (5 miles).

Maps: OS Landranger 195 Bournemouth, Purbeck and surrounding area. Map ref: SY 999 788.

Degree of difficulty: The walk includes some stone stiles and grassy paths which are slippery when wet.

How to get there: Follow the A351 through Corfe Castle and on the western outskirts of Swanage turn right on to the B3069.

Parking: Roadside parking in the village.

Pub facilities: The King's Arms, Langton Matravers, is a free house on the main road through the village and, like most other buildings here, is built of locally-quarried Purbeck stone. It is also a genuine smugglers' pub – at least one 19th century landlord was in league with the smugglers and many an illicit operation was planned within these walls (see History section).

The King's Arms offers a range of beers, including three or four real ales. The menu includes lunchtime snacks (and full meals on request) and and evening meals, with much of the food home-made. The walled beer garden is pleasant and sheltered and barbecues are often held there on Saturdays.

Opening times: 11.30 am-3 pm, 6.30-11 pm Monday-Saturday (and sometimes through the afternoon on Saturday), 12 noon-3 pm and 7-10.30 pm Sunday. Tel: 01929 422979.

Other attractions: The Coach House Museum, which is dedicated to the local stone industry. Open April to mid-October, 10 am-12 noon and 2-4 pm, or at other times by appointment (closed Sundays). Tel: 01929 423168 to speak to the curator.

History: Like its larger neighbours Worth Matravers and Swanage, Langton Matravers in the old days was a village which earned its living mainly from the rock beneath its foundations. Quarrying was the dominant industry and generations of menfolk spent most of their lives hacking away at the local stone. But like the fishermen of other coastal villages and the labourers of agricultural Dorset, many also welcomed the opportunity to increase their incomes with a little smuggling – and often more than a little. Usually they had to look no further than the honeycombed quarries they worked in for a suitable place to store their contraband.

"Here, as in Durlston Bay, the coastguards' work was very difficult," wrote the Purbeck smuggling historian W.M. Hardy early in the present century. "Most of the smugglers were quarrymen, and therefore had business in these lurking places. They knew all the roads and paths, rocks and footholds, and could run about the cliffs as easily and safely as goats, whereas the coastguards, in patrolling the cliffs, kept to their narrow track along the edge, clearly defined by a dotted line of whitewashed stones for their guidance at night."

The King's Arms, Langton Matravers

A report from Poole Custom House in 1804 into the state of smuggling locally speaks of goods being "very frequently landed" on this section of the Purbeck coast and "immediately concealed in the stone quarries where, from their great number and extent, it is wholly impossible to discover them". The report identifies the main landing places between Durlston and St Alban's Head as Dancing Ledge, Seacombe and Winspit – in other words, the only places where the steepness of the Purbeck cliffs did not make landings virtually impossible.

"At the first place [Dancing Ledge]," says the report, "neither carriages nor horses can approach the shore nearer than half-a-mile, in consequence of which small quantities only are landed and which are conveyed from boats to the carriages by the smugglers themselves. At Seacombe, about one mile from Dancing Ledge, horses are made use of and the goods conveyed directly from the shore and secreted in caves in the stone quarries. One mile from Seacombe is Winspit and here horses are made use of and the goods moved as from Seacombe."

By 1830, according to W.M. Hardy, the Coastguard had discovered most of the Langton smugglers' regular hiding places and it became necessary to look for alternatives. In their search for a solution, they turned to the church, and their prayers were quickly answered. "Over the ceiling of the church will be a capital place," suggested one seasoned smuggler. "The coastguards will never dream of it there."

For a long time, indeed, the coastguards did not dream of it and many cargoes found their way up through the tower and into the roof space of the recently rebuilt St George's Church. One Victorian native of Langton Matravers, Charles W.T. Dean, recalled being posted outside the church as a look-out by his grandfather, the village sub-Postmaster Charles Hayward. The year was 1869 and young Charles was ten years old and recovering from illness. He was instructed to walk up and down and "not look too involved with anything particular" and to alert his grandfather (who would be inside the church) if a Peeler policeman came near.

"Seven gentlemen arrived variously to meet my grandfather, and they all went inside the church," wrote Dean. "A Peeler came down from Garfield, past me, and thence on to Stepps. I had given the alert (taking my cap off, shaking it, and putting it on again) and whilst the Peeler walked by all was silent in the church, nor any light. Presently came two stone carts from Garfield end, and the seven gentlemen came out and assisted the drivers with unloading the stones. These were stacked flat-down and not up-down. The men then brought in barrels of all sizes and different shapes. All together this went into the church – I could not see where, but I heard a bell make a half-sounding, and heard a man say something bad. They then, I think, came to the porch, and the two drivers took papers from my grandfather, re-loaded the stone and drove off to Stepps. I heard much talking; my grandfather came out to me, thanked me profusely for my assistance, and gave me a gold coin."

W.M. Hardy gives a detailed account of what, according to his information, may have been the last occasion that contraband was stored in Langton church. The smuggled spirits were landed at Dancing Ledge and, due to an unexpected shortage of manpower, stored initially at Spyway Barton, hidden under piles of straw and guarded by a bull whose ferocity was guaranteed to deter even the most courageous coastguard.

The next stage of the operation was planned the following evening in a private room at the King's Arms, whose landlord was sympathetic to the cause. It was decided to avoid the front entrance to the church, which was considered too risky. Instead the goods would be taken through the garden of a big house called Durnford and into the church through a small door in the west wall. The publican agreed to deal with the Durnford gardener, who had a weakness for a tipple; a shepherd offered part

A milestone on the Priest's Way

of a dead sheep to silence the Durnford dog.

On the next night again the smugglers met at Spyway, loaded a wagon with the tubs, covered them with straw and drove to the back of Durnford. The plan went like clockwork and the goods were safely lodged in the church. But any celebrations by the smugglers would have been premature. Three weeks later, before the goods could be despatched to their eventual destination, the Poole Collector of Customs was mysteriously tipped off about the hidden haul – perhaps by a smuggler tempted by the £50 reward. The officer duly swooped, chalking the arrow denoting "seized goods" on each tub and returning next day to collect them.

"I have never heard that the sacrilege was repeated, and the church ever used again as sanctuary for smuggled goods," adds Hardy.

Another tale associated with the King's Arms concerns the daughter of a late 18th century landlord, William Marshfield. In later life the old lady would tell how she came to be born on top of two barrels of smuggled brandy! The great event followed an illicit landing at Dancing Ledge and the delivery of two barrels to the pub, where the usual practice was quickly to transfer the contents to English bottles and burn the incriminating barrels. On this occasion there had been no time to remove the bungs when a message arrived informing Marshfield that the Customs men were about to arrive. At this the quick-thinking landlord asked the two smugglers to bring the barrels upstairs to the bedroom where a midwife was attending his wife in expectation of an imminent birth. The barrels were put under the bed, the bedclothes pulled down to conceal them and the midwife and mother-to-be instructed to put on a good show if they wished to save the

Dancing Ledge

baby's father from prison.

Despite the protests of the midwife and the convincing screams of her patient, the officers were determined to search the room and forced their way in. But their search was conducted with haste and some embarrassment and without approaching the noisy woman's bed. In this way the brandy tubs were saved from seizure and William Marshfield from jail. And that's not all. For the stress and drama of the incident served to induce the birth, which took place almost immediately and before the barrels could be removed from under the bed.

The Walk: From the pub, walk up the hill. On the right is St George's Close where you will find the Coach House Museum (see Other Attractions above).

Opposite the church (used as a hiding place by 19th century smugglers), turn left into Durnford Drove, following the footpath sign to Dancing Ledge.

At the end of Durnford Drove go through the white gate and straight along the track. There is a dry stone wall on the left and trees on the right.

Where the tarmac ends, carry straight on along the path and through the gate. Pass the National Trust sign for Spyway Barn and after a short distance go through a second gate.

Walk straight on, and when you come to a crossroads of tracks, turn left on to the Priest's Way. This ancient track along the limestone ridgeway is supposed to derive its name from the fact that in the Middle Ages priests from the mother church at Worth Matravers used it to reach the young settlement at Swanage.

Go up the slope and through the gate. There are views to the left of Ballard and Nine Barrow Downs.

Ignore the stile and sign on the right towards Dancing Ledge, and stay on the Priest's Way. After a pleasant walk downhill between hedgerows, go through the gate and round the corner, keeping the wall to your right.

Follow the track as it curves to the left

around the edge of a field. Go over the cattle grid and turn right on to the bridleway.

Walk up the slope past the signpost marked "Swanage 1 mile". Go along the track and through a gate which has a stone "Priest's Way" sign inset into the wall beside it.

Walk to the next gate which has stone steps beside it, and once on the other side, carry on along the track.

On reaching another gate, go through, and cross the field (at the time of writing it has one gate across the path), keeping the fence on your left.

At the far end of the meadow cross the stile by the gate. To your left is Bellevue Farm, which is private property. Turn right, following the stone sign marked "Coast 1 mile".

As you walk up the rise, look behind you for good views over Langton Matravers.

Go through the gate which is across the path. Continue to the end of the track, where you will see a gate and stone stile.

On the other side, cross the field to the wooden gate and stile.

Go past the National Trust "Belle Vue" sign, and after a short distance, turn right at the stone sign, marked "Upper Path Dancing Ledge".

Head across the grass to the steps in the wall beside the stone which points towards Dancing Ledge.

Walk straight across to the next stone wall, keeping the sea on your left. There is a stone seat if you want to stop to admire the view.

Cross the stile beside the gate and go on to the next stile, which is set in the stone wall. Climb over, and follow the path over some rough ground.

At the top of the rise you will have a good view to St Alban's Head. After some distance the next stile carries a notice saying that the path beyond this point is not a public right of way but that the owner allows it to be used.

Follow the track down the slope to the stone wall, turn left, and follow the wall to a gap in the hedge.

Once through the gap, cross the corner of the field to another gap, on the other side of which is a wooden signpost.

Bear right, and keeping the sea on your left, follow the track across the grass towards the cliff.

Cross the next stile and pass the National Trust's "Spyway Farm" sign.

There is an excellent view down to Dancing Ledge and the caves are clearly visible. Countless cargoes were illegally landed on the rocky ledge in the 18th and 19th centuries.

Once over the stepping stones of a small stream, you will soon arrive at the clifftop over Dancing Ledge. There are often parties of rockclimbers here, but for the less adventurous there are steps down to the beach!

At the end of the wall near the top of the steps, follow the sign towards Spyway Barn. The path is steep, and climbs diagonally.

At the top there are good views along the coast and out to sea.

Go through the gate, and follow the stone sign marked "Spyway and Langton 1 mile".

The grassy track goes through the farmyard at Spyway Barn, where the information boards are well worth a look. Follow the sign to Langton, and you will soon cross the Priest's Way and be able to retrace your steps to the village.

Walk No: 11 THE SMUGGLERS' CHURCH Kinson-Longham

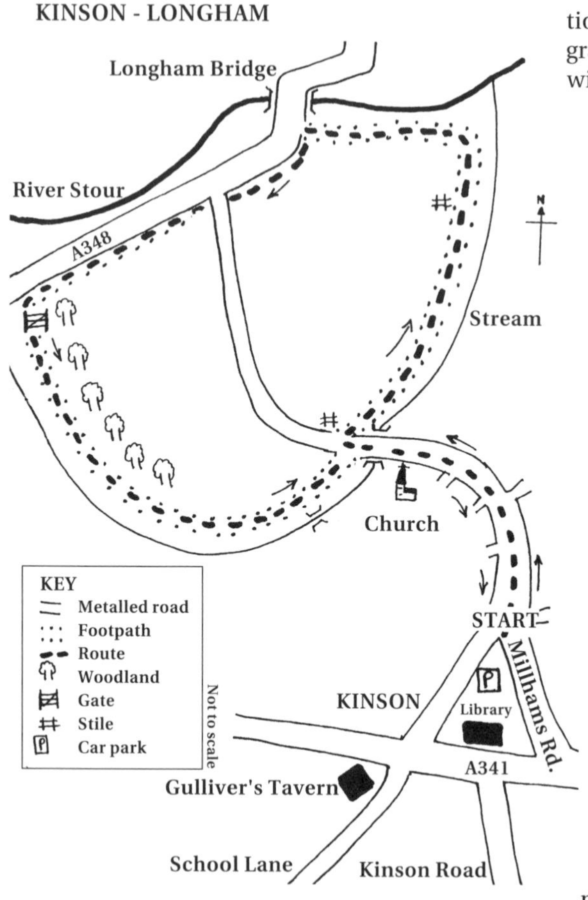

Distance: 3 kms (1.9 miles)

Maps: OS Landranger 195 Bournemouth, Purbeck and surrounding area. Map ref: SZ 069 966.

Bournemouth Street Plan (Estate Publications Red Book).

Degree of difficulty: This is an exceptionally easy walk on grass or metalled road, with no hills and only two stiles. Most of it is across public open space and the route is extremely simple.

How to get there: Kinson lies on the A341 between Bear Cross and Northbourne. Gulliver's Tavern is in the middle of Kinson on the main road.

Parking: Gulliver's Tavern has a car park which patrons are welcome to use. There is also a free public car park behind the library opposite, entered from Millhams Road.

Pub facilities: Gulliver's Tavern, formerly the Dolphin, is a spacious olde-worlde pub with atmosphere. It dates from the 18th century and has smuggling traditions from the same era, when Kinson was a major contraband centre. It has been refurbished within the last few years and renamed after Isaac Gulliver, who is said to haunt the place and who certainly would have frequented it when he lived

Gulliver's Tavern, Kinson

at Kinson (see History section). The pub is also reputed to be connected to the church and other buildings by tunnels. A notable landlord from the 20th century was middle distance runner Charles Bennett, winner of Britain's first ever Olympic track and field gold medal in Paris in 1900, when he also broke two world records.

Gulliver's Tavern is a free house serving bar snacks and a range of drinks which include real ales. Entertainment includes live music on Friday, Saturday and Sunday. There is also a beer garden and car park for patrons.

Opening times: 12 noon-3 pm and 7-11 pm Monday-Saturday, 12 noon-3 pm and 7-10.30 pm Sunday. Tel: 01202 580739.

History: It is not for nothing that St Andrew's Church, Kinson, is tradtionally known as "the smugglers' church". For most of the 18th and much of the 19th century, this old village on Bourne Heath (now the seaside town of Bournemouth) was a hotbed of smugglers, and they considered the church and churchyard as part of their domain.

Near the south door of the church is a chest tomb used by generations of smugglers as a hiding place for contraband. Apparently the tomb had a pivoted stone at one end which could be moved to facilitate the insertion or removal of smuggled goods. The church tower was another storage place. So many tubs of brandy were hauled up the outside of the tower over the years that the ropes wore grooves in the stonework at the top. These remained clearly visible until restoration work in the 1930s.

On the north side of the church is a famous smuggler's grave, with an inscription which vividly illustrates the popular view of the time that smuggling was at best a legitimate business activity and at worst a minor misdemeanour. It reads:

To the Memory of
ROBERT TROTMAN
Late of Rond [Rowde] in the County
of Wilts who was barbarously
Murder'd on the Shore near
Poole the 24 March 1765

A little Tea one leaf I did not steal
For Guiltless Blood shed I to GOD appeal
Put Tea in one scale human Blood in tother
And think what tis to slay thy harmless Brother

An inquest jury was similarly disposed, recording a verdict of "wilful murder by persons unknown". Such were the views of the smuggling community but the Poole Customs Collector's report on Trotman's death offers a different perspective. It records that Trotman was "the head of a desperate gang of smugglers", 20 in number, who attempted to load a large quantity of freshly-landed tea on to their horses on the beach between Sandbanks and Bournemouth. The operation was interrupted by Lieutenant Down, Commander of the Royal Navy cutter *Folkestone*, who at 11 pm led a 15-strong landing party on to the beach.

One of his men, Midshipman Robert Wilson, jumped on to one of the horses and rode in among the smugglers to declare a seizure but was immediately pulled to the ground and beaten about the head and body with the solid ends of horsewhips. Lieutenant Down's clerk, Edward Morrice, was similarly beaten and slightly wounded by a pistol shot which grazed his chest. The smugglers "then dragged him into the sea" and left him to drown, but "with great difficulty he crawled out and got into one of the chines, where he concealed himself till the dispute was over".

"At this juncture Mr Down with his other hands came up and got in amongst them and he declared that if anyone offered to carry away any of the tea he would fire at them, on which some that had their horses loaded endeavoured to get off, when he gave orders to his men to hamstring their horses and cut off the bags of tea from them." At this, the smugglers again laid into the Navy men with their whips and fired two pistols, shooting Able Seaman Atkins in the leg. The report does not say at what stage Down's men opened fire but there was obviously a two-way exchange of shots which killed not only Trotman but nine of the smugglers' horses. The remaining smugglers managed to escape with part of their cargo.

The great Isaac Gulliver lived at Kinson for some time and owned several properties in the village. They included a shop with adjoining malthouse and cellars, where he traded openly in wine and spirits. The business itself was legal and above board; we can only guess as to whether the same could be said of the way the stock was acquired.

One of Gulliver's houses at Kinson was Howe Lodge, an elegant Georgian dwelling in Brook Road, which was demolished in 1958. Features included a secret room entered through a special door concealed ten feet up a chimney, and a brick-built tunnel leading away from a cellar, itself entered via a trapdoor in the dining room. According to legend, it was in this house that Gulliver feigned death to escape arrest. Forewarned that a search party was on its way, he whitened his faced with chalk,

St Andrew's Kinson ... 'the smugglers' church'

climbed into an open coffin in an alcove under the stairs and managed to convince his unwelcome visitors that their problems were over at last.

Gulliver's property also included Manor Farm and the site now occupied by Pelhams. The present Pelhams, now a community centre, was built about 1816 by Gulliver's son-in-law William Fryer, a member of a wealthy banking family. But there was an earlier Pelhams on the site in the late 18th century, when Gulliver himself was the owner. It may have been the "neat and convenient dwelling house with suitable offices and good stable for horses, necessary outhouses, etc", referred to in a newspaper advertisement in 1788, when "Mr Gulliver" was named as the owner and a Mr Tait as the tenant.

In his heyday Gulliver controlled a vast network of smugglers which extended throughout the length and breadth of Dorset and beyond. At Kinson his men included John Singer, who in 1777 was said to have "long been concerned in the smuggling trade". A large haul of contraband was seized from Singer's granary in that year. It included 541 gallons of brandy and rum and 1,871 lbs of raw coffee. It was one of several major seizures from Kinson and Longham in the 1770s and '80s.

The records of Dorchester Prison provide evidence that Kinson retained its smuggling link well into the 19th century. Five Kinson smugglers are listed between 1809 and 1828, four of them in the last three years of that period.

Stories abound at Kinson of secret tunnels and underground passages. One resident, interviewed for a book published in 1972, remembered being taken as a child in the '50s into a "a tunnel of sorts", entered on the Longham side of St Andrew's Church. He thought this probably came up in or close to the church. Later he was taken to Gulliver's house in Brook Road and entered another tunnel. "We were told that it led eventually

Smuggler Robert Trotman's gravestone in Kinson churchyard

to routes to Poole and Christchurch harbour." Both tunnels were about 3 ft 6 ins high and fitted at intervals with air vents. "When a tunnel approached a building it widened into a small chamber."

The Walk: On leaving the public car park turn left into Millhams Road and pass Pelhams on your right. These days the former home of Isaac Gulliver's relatives is a well-used community centre set in a large park with tennis courts and swings, slides and a paddling pool for children.

A little further along Millhams Road, on an ancient site among the trees, is the "smugglers' church", St Andrew's. In the churchyard can be seen Robert Trotman's gravestone and, near the main door, the chest tomb where contraband used to be stored.

Continue along Millhams Road, cross the bridge and take the unmarked path to the right, over the stile.

Walk along the riverside track, keeping the stream on your right. Depending on the season, you may see swans or coots in the bullrushes.

The wooded Iron Age hillfort of Dudsbury will soon come into view, across the water meadows on the other side of the River Stour. This area used to be known as "Hillams" and in an old legal document dated 1812, Kinson-born William Lockyer refers to having worked as a "yearly servant to Mr Isaac Gulliver at Hillam Lands" around 1780.

Cross the stile and stay on the path, which leads to the south bank of the Stour, looking out for the vivid flash of a kingfisher, which can sometimes be seen against the grey background of Longham Bridge as the traffic roars by.

The path leads to the bridge, where there is access on to the main Ringwood Road. Turn left on to the pavement and head away from the bridge.

After a short distance the path goes behind a tall hedge and is screened from the busy road. Despite the proximity of the traffic, the bushes are varied and well-laden. In autumn there are rose hips, haws and even hops.

Where the hedge ends, and the path reverts to pavement, go through the wooden gate which you will see on the left. There is a signpost marked "Dudsbury one and three quarters".

The path goes straight on and is wide and grassy. This very pleasant stretch has tall willows on the left, and a stream on the right. There are kingfishers here, too, darting through the rushes; also seats for those who wish to linger awhile.

Soon the square tower of St Andrew's Church comes into view and shortly afterwards the path rejoins Millhams Road.

Turn right on to the road and walk past the church back to the car park.

WHITE WIGS AND OTHERS
Lyme Regis

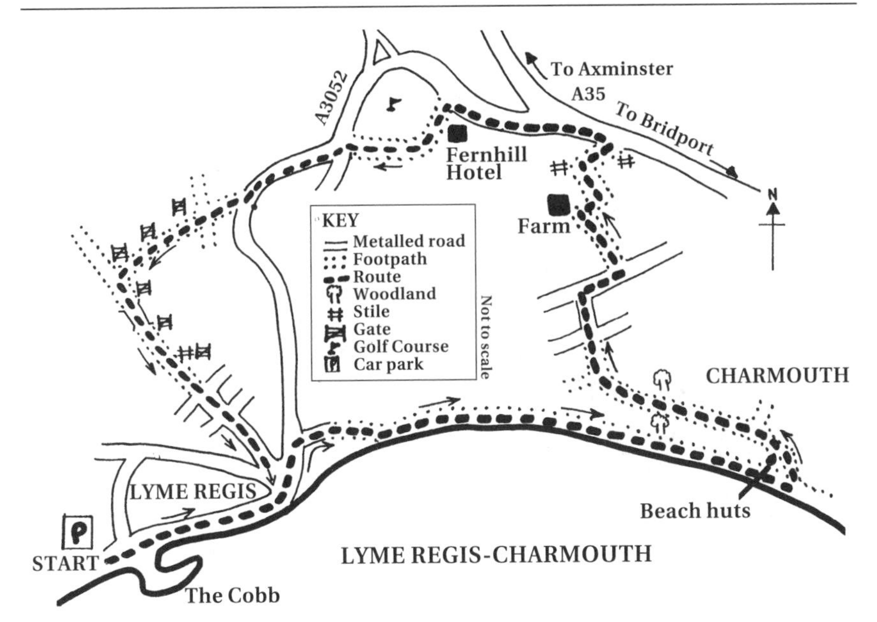

Two walks have been provided at Lyme Regis — a town trail, designed to capture the flavour of this old Regency seaside town, and a much longer walk, taking in the neighbouring village of Charmouth, spectacular views from the clifftop, a contrastingly leafy river valley and even a brief excursion to Devon!

Distance: Longer walk 11 kms (6.9 miles); shorter walk 3.2 kms (2 miles).

Maps: OS Landranger 193 Taunton & Lyme Regis.
Map ref: SY 338 916.

Degree of difficulty: The longer walk includes steep unfenced cliff paths and a golf course, making it unsuitable for very young children.

Important: At the time of writing the Heritage Coast Path is blocked by cliff falls, so the outward route leads along the beach. *To avoid being cut off, this route should only be attempted on a falling tide. Before setting out, check tide times carefully with the Lyme Tourist Information Centre (tel 01297 442138).*

The walk should also not be attempted during a wet spell because of the danger of mud flows on to the beach.

How to get there: Lyme Regis is Dorset's most westerly town and is reached from the east by taking the A35 and A 3052. Follow the main road through the town and turn left off Pound Street along Cobb Road (see map). At the bottom of the hill, turn right. The car park is a short distance further on.

The Cobb Arms, Lyme Regis

Parking: West of the Cobb at Monmouth Beach (pay and display).

Pub facilities: The Cobb Arms is the nearest pub to the car park. It is a Palmers pub and was built in 1937, although there was another pub of the same name in the more distant past which now survives as a private house two doors away in Cobb Road. In the present Cobb Arms, enlarged historical photographs of Lyme decorate the walls. There are two outdoor terraces, including the tiny Sea View Terrace, which overlooks the Cobb and Lyme Bay and offers fine views to Portland. In dry weather it is also an ideal place to sit and watch the world go by!

The pub has a particularly varied and interesting menu which includes such dishes as smuggler's fish pie and, for the children, turkey dinosaur with beans and chips! Portions are generous and reasonably priced and half-a-dozen vegetarian dishes are also offered. Drinks include four real ales. Accommodation is also available in three twin-bed rooms.

Opening times: 10 am-11 pm Monday-Saturday, 11 am-10.30 pm Sunday (all year round). Tel: 01297 443242.

There are numerous cafes, tea shops, restaurants and other pubs in the area, including the **Harbour Inn** and the **Royal Standard** nearby and the **Rock Point Inn** and the **Pilot Boat** at the other end of Marine Parade.

The Pilot Boat beside the River Lym in Bridge Street is managed by the same family as the Cobb Arms but is a much older building with its own smuggling connection (see History section). This pub is open from 11 am-11 pm Monday-Saturday and 12 noon-10.30 pm Sunday and serves quality meals all day with fresh fish and vegetarian dishes both specialities. Tel: 01297 443157.

Other attractions: There are many including the **Philpot Museum** in Bridge

View of the Cobb and Lyme Bay

Street, which houses a fine fossil collection. Tel: 01297 443370.

History: A visitor to Lyme Regis 200 years ago might have noticed a large group of men hanging around the beach and dressed in strikingly similar garb. "A smuggler named Gulliver," wrote the Lyme historian George Roberts within 12 years of Isaac Gulliver's death in 1822, "kept 40 or 50 men constantly employed, who wore a kind of livery, powdered hair, and smock frocks, from which they obtained the name of the White Wigs. These men kept together, and would not allow a few officers to take what they were carrying."

The wearing of what amounted to a uniform seems a strange habit for smugglers who might be expected to try to avoid attention rather than than court it. There is a simple explanation, however. By ordering his men to wear smock frocks and long powdered hair, Gulliver was making them appear as the respectable servants of some wealthy landowner rather than as a bunch of ruffians. It was a policy in keeping with Gulliver's image of himself. He was known as — and happy to be known as — the Gentle Smuggler and he boasted that no revenue officer had ever died at the hands of his men. He was immensely proud of his success, and would have been prouder still to know that he is so well remembered 200 years later. According to George Roberts, he even "employed lawyers to arrange his affairs so that all who should take any benefit from his fortune should bear the name of Gulliver".

At Lyme Regis, Gulliver's men usually gathered on the beach near the point where the River Lym joins the sea. In those days there was a chamber facing the sea, where the White Wigs would take refreshment and "remain in waiting till their services were required". The chamber was less than 100 yards from the Custom House. Within the last few years, refurbishment work at the nearby Pilot Boat, an old coaching inn in Bridge Street, uncovered some steps leading down not to a cellar but to the wall of the River Lym. It would be hard to believe that smugglers were not the main users of the steps. There is also reputed to be a tunnel under nearby Buddles Bridge.

The vagaries of import regulations as applied to Lyme often worked in the smugglers' favour. During his visits to the port in the early 1680s, Treasury investigator William Culliford noted that although ships unloaded at the small man-made harbour known as the Cobb, the Customs men were not entitled to check the goods until they reached the Cobb Gate half-a-mile away. Often, the imports never reached the Cobb Gate at all as merchants took advantage of the "many places and ways between the Cobb and Cobb Gate" to disappear by another route and avoid payment of duties. Even those who did attend the Cobb Gate sometimes found it unmanned, in which case their horses "shall slip into the town, and the duty is wholly lost".

Despite Culliford's comments, little changed at Lyme and 100 years after his visits the town's smugglers were still enjoying "a latitude that will scarcely be credited", as George Roberts puts it. He wrote of Lyme in 1780: "Nothing could be seized above high-water mark; so that pipes of wine have actually been landed close to the Custom House at Lyme, then at the bottom of the town, and allowed to remain on the beach and Cobb Gate leading to the Custom House!"

The records of Lyme Regis Quarters Sessions give details of many contraband seizures in the 1720s, '30s and '40s. They usually involved relatively small quantities of brandy, rum, wine, tea, tobacco or chocolate, which had generally been hidden or abandoned on beaches, among rocks or in hedges, ditches, barns and outhouses. Captured tobacco was usually burnt in a lime kiln on the Cobb. According to George Roberts, the kiln was often completely full and "each of the assembled bye-standers had an opportunity of stuffing his pockets full". He adds: "At length the fire was applied, and the flavour could be sniffed at a great distance to leeward by the hardy mariner, who deplored such a waste of this cherished commodity."

In the case of seized contraband other than tobacco, the Customs service first had to give the owners of the goods a chance to claim them. If they failed to do so (which was usually the case) they would later be auctioned at one of several venues in Lyme, three of which were the Guildhall, the Three Cups Inn and Susanna Webber's coffee house. There was also a seizure at the Three Cups in 1731, when Indian silk handkerchiefs were discovered in someone's saddlebags in an outhouse.

Many sons of Lyme Regis (and quite a few daughters) grew up to be smugglers but the town also produced one of the greatest contraband captors in history. Warren Lisle, son of Lyme's Collector of Customs, George Lisle, makes his first appearance in legal documents as a teenager in 1719, when he was ordered to make regular maintenance payments for his illegitimate son! It was an inauspicious introduction to the courtroom, but things could only get better. He went on to become Captain Lisle, owner of several privateer cutters which cruised the coastal waters of southern England in a relentless search for smugglers and smuggled goods. In the course of his career, Lisle seized contraband worth an astonishing £520,000! He also earned the respect of smugglers and Customs men alike. In retirement at Weymouth in 1782, he found himself advising none other than the Prime Minister, Lord Shelburne, on the state of smuggling and revenue collection in the south. He reported that the crews of Dorset and Devon revenue cutters "content themselves with a small share from the smugglers and suffer the greater part to be run ashore". Most of the lower ranking land-based Customs officers were corrupt and "often assist in running and bringing ashore large quantities, without payment of duties, for which they receive large gratuities and live like gentlemen in their house".

Lyme's smuggling ships at this time included several of 100 tons, known as "tonnagers". They habitually carried documents made out as if they were en route from Cherbourg to Ostend. George Roberts records that one tonnager was boarded off the Cobb on one occasion and found to be full of wine. Next day she entered the Cobb and was found to have not a single pipe of wine on board. The Collector of Customs, Mr Raymond, decided to seize her anyway on the grounds that she could not have sailed to Ostend and back in one night. In court, however, the smugglers claimed they had thrown the cargo overboard to prevent the vessel from sinking. They even bribed a Customs man to say that he had feared for his life when he boarded the vessel, and it was his evidence that swayed the case in their favour.

Lyme also features in the published memoirs of the Devon-born smuggler Jack Rattenbury, who writes of having "pretty good success" with a small smuggling vessel sailing between Lyme and the Channel Islands.

The greatest blow struck against the smugglers was the formation of the Coastguard, or Preventive Service, in the 1820s. Suddenly the contraband trades had to contend with teams of well-armed, well-trained navy personnel patrolling the clifftops and cutters cruising offshore. Lyme was given its own Coastguard station and incidents inevitably followed. One occurred near the river mouth at Charmouth in 1825 when three men of the Lyme Preventive Station captured 150 kegs and two men. Within minutes they were under attack by a gang of 70 or 80 liquor-crazed smugglers, who "advanced with great violence" and tried to cut one officer's throat. The officers opened fire and wounded one smuggler, who was carried away by his colleagues. The smugglers then bombarded the officers with large stones thrown from the clifftop, causing severe cuts and bruises to all three.

The Longer Walk: Leave the car park and head east towards the Cobb, which can be explored if time permits.

Walk along the beach or the Marine Parade. Both give fine views of the Cobb, and of the coastline to the east.

At the end of Marine Parade you will be near the spot where Isaac Gulliver's men gathered, waiting to be called into action. Carry on along the sea front, past the museum and on to the beach.

There is a large notice board warning walkers that they can be cut off by the incoming tide. *Please take care!*

The Royal Standard, Lyme Regis

Head east towards Charmouth, past the rock pools and fossil hunters. You will have a good view of Golden Cap ahead and Lyme Regis behind.

On reaching Charmouth, take the path at the end of the row of beach huts before the cafe. It leads back up the cliff, and is marked with a stone indicating "Cliff path to Lyme Regis".

At the top of the cliff, follow the path signposted Lyme Regis.

The track climbs, giving excellent views to Charmouth beach, Golden Cap and even Portland on a clear day.

Pass a seat, and keep walking uphill. There are houses on the right. Near the top is a sign marking Black Venn, owned by the National Trust. At the time of writing a cliff fall has closed this part of the Dorset Coast Path and an alternative route has been posted, which is described here.

The path leads into woodland and turns inland between houses. On the left is one called Templewood. Cross the road, and go straight on at the wooden signpost marked "Lyme Regis" — alongside a house called Foxley Dene.

Walk along the narrow metalled lane which enjoys excellent views over the coast and countryside to the north.

At the junction with another lane, where there is a wooden signpost, walk in the direction of Charmouth village. A short way along take the turning on the left, opposite a house called South Molle.

The track leads across a field, and you will see the bypass below you to the right. Bear right through the farmyard, following the yellow arrows, and climb the stile at the end.

Turn right across the field towards the wooden pole with the yellow sign on it, and head down the slope to the stile beside the road junction where the A35 and A3052 meet.

Once over the stile, go down the steps and turn left taking the road to Lyme Regis. This is quite safe for pedestrians as there is a pavement.

Walk up the hill, and just past the Fernhill Hotel on the left, take the footpath marked by a wooden signpost. It leads into woodland and up a slope.

At the top go straight on, following the sign for Lyme Regis golf club which warns people to look out for golf balls.

Cross the golf course, following the white marker stones, and turn left on to the main road. There is a pavement for walkers.

At the junction bear right, staying on the main road. On reaching the "bends" road sign, cross over and follow the gravel track down the slope. At the time of writing there was a sign — "Coppers Cottages" on the gate.

This is a particularly peaceful area, with views over the valley to Rhode Barton on the right. The path leads downhill.

At the bottom of the hill continue through the gate opposite and into a field.

Cross the field, keeping the hedge on your right, and the overhead power lines to your left. At the bottom of the field, go through the gate, and straight on down the next field.

Go through the gate to the right of the sewage works, and walk downhill along the gravel track.

Where our track joins another at the picturesque old mill, turn left beside the stream and step into Devon!

Go through the gate marked with a yellow arrow, straight across the wooden bridge over the River Lym, and through the gate at the other end, back into Dorset.

Keep to the left across the field, negotiate the gate or stile (which are side by side) and continue over the bridge.

Follow the track, and at the road go straight across into Windsor Terrace. This is a very pleasant riverside walk back into Lyme Regis, with interesting cottages, and ducks everywhere — on lawns and doorsteps as well as snoozing on the footpath!

Walk straight across at the next junction, into Jericho, and follow the stream, turning right at its end back into Lyme.

The Lyme Regis Town Trail: The town offers much to see at any time of the year. It is most famous for its picturesque, man-made harbour, dating from the reign of Edward I and known as the Cobb. It was Edward who gave Lyme its first charter in 1284 and its Regis title.

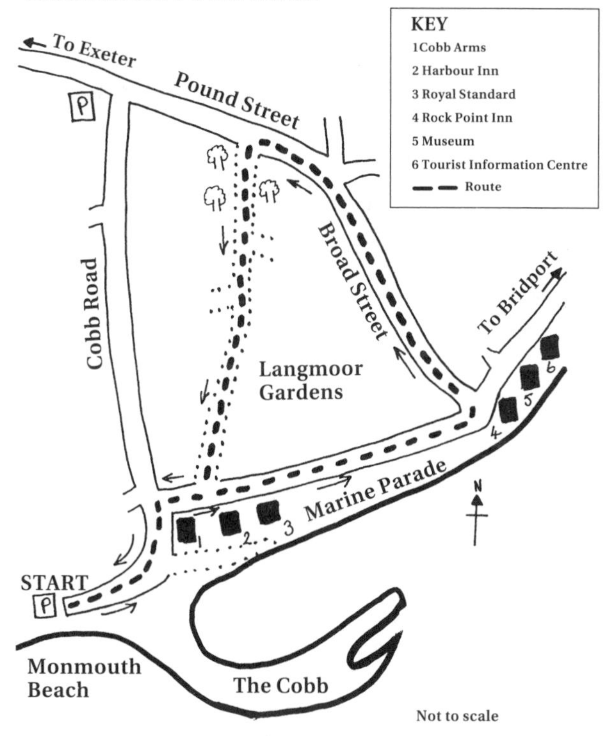

The town has a rich geological heritage and has been famous for its fossils since a young girl called Mary Anning discovered the skeleton of an icthyosaur in 1811. She became known as the Fossil Woman of Lyme and today fossils are a common sight in Lyme's shops and museums.

There are also literary connections, most notably through the novels Persuasion (by Jane Austen, who stayed here for a time) and The French Lieutenant's Woman (by John Fowles, who still lives here).

Our walk around Lyme is about two miles long and gives superb views of the town, and a chance to walk the steep narrow streets with their Georgian buildings, which date from an era when, like Weymouth some miles to the east, the town was a prosperous watering place.

From the Monmouth Beach car park, head towards the artificial harbour known as the Cobb, which has witnessed much in its long history, including the landing of the Duke of Monmouth and his rebels in 1685.

From the Cobb, walk along Marine Parade. Traffic is prohibited here and on the first stretch there are shops and pubs on both sides.

Just past Lyme Potters, the promenade opens out to give views from the Cobb to Golden Cap and even Portland on a clear day.

The cottages along the Parade are all different, and painted in pastel colours. Look out for the thatched ones, and the ornate guttering.

At the end of Marine Parade is the Rock Point Inn. If you want to visit the Tourist Information Centre or the Philpot Museum with its excellent fossil collection, carry straight on along the road. Both are a little way up the hill on the right. The Pilot Boat, an old coaching inn with its own smuggling connection (see History section), is also in this vicinity in Bridge Street.

To continue our trail, turn left at the end of Marine Parade. To the left at the top of the steps are the cannons, last fired in 1690 at the French.

The steep hilly street is lined with interesting gift shops, delicatessans, cafes and galleries.

On the left is the old Three Cups Inn (now closed), where in the 18th century seized contraband was often sold by auction.

At the top of the hill the road bears left. Just past the New Haven Hotel on the left, go through the gates into Langmoor Gardens.

Pass the well-kept borders and you will soon have a panoramic view of Lyme Bay before you. This is the best vantage point for the Cobb, and from here there is a choice of paths past the putting green and back down to Marine Parade.

THE SMUGGLERS' COVE
Lulworth and the Cove

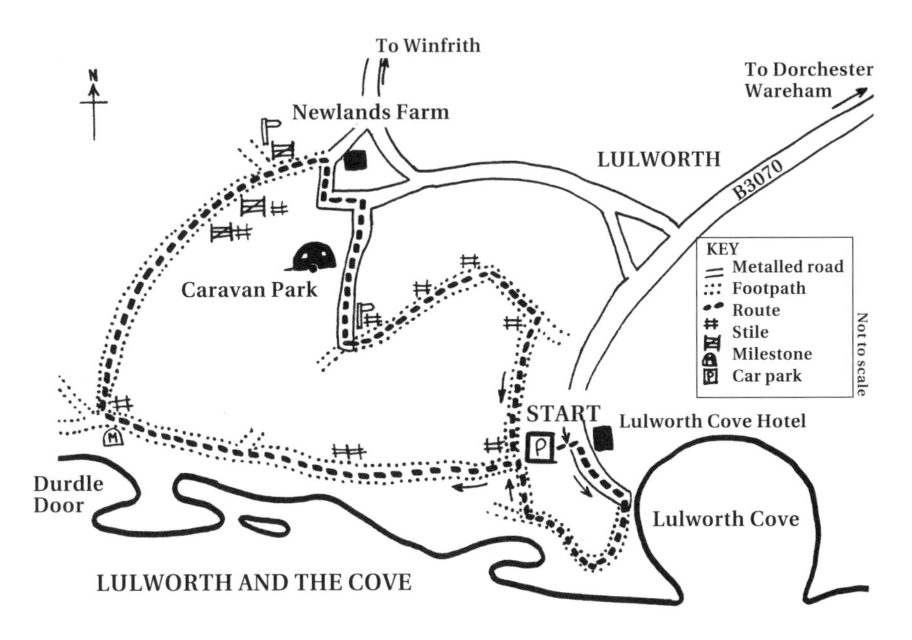

Distance: 5.6 kms (3.5 miles)

Maps: OS Landranger 194 Dorchester, Weymouth and surrounding area. Map ref: SY 822 801.

Degree of difficulty: This walk has everything! It takes in some of the finest coastal scenery in Britain in an area of such geological importance and interest that people come from all over England and overseas to study it.

In contrast, the route, when it turns inland, passes through a green and peaceful valley, so sheltered that even the sound of the sea is lost.

There is one steep climb, which can be seen from the car park. As some of the walk is along unfenced cliffs, it is not suitable for young children or unleashed dogs. In wet weather the cliff paths are slippery.

How to get there: Lulworth Cove lies due south of Wool, a village on the A352 between Dorchester and Wareham.

Parking: The Lulworth Cove Hotel has a small car park but walkers are advised to use the large public car park opposite, which has an all day fixed charge.

Pub facilities: The Lulworth Cove Hotel is a large and spacious free house with games room and garden, a comprehensive menu of restaurant meals and bar food. Drinks include two real ales which are changed from time to time and a selection of lagers, bitters, draught cider, etc. The hotel has no car park of its own but stands opposite the large public car

The Lulworth Cove Hotel

park where charges vary according to the season. Accommodation is available and guests in the 15 rooms are provided with tickets for the car park.

Opening times: Summer 11.30 am-11 pm Monday-Saturday, 12 noon-10.30 pm Sunday; winter 12 noon-3 pm, 7.30-11 pm Monday-Saturday, 12 noon-3 pm, 7.30-10.30 pm Sunday. Tel: 01929 400333.

The Castle, north of the village on the B3070, used to be called the Jolly Sailor and was a favourite haunt of smugglers.

Optional extras: Camera and binoculars.

Other attractions: The Lulworth Cove Heritage Centre beside the car park includes permanent exhibitions on smuggling, paddle steamers, the Dorset oil industry and country wines.

The Information Centre near the start of the walk offers many informative leaflets that may be of interest.

There are several hotels open to non-residents, a cafe overlooking the sea, a pebble beach and a bay popular with divers.

History: Lulworth's sheltered cove, coupled with its general remoteness, made it a favourite haunt of smugglers, who were active here for centuries, and not only in import smuggling. Back in the 16th century, hundreds of horses left Lulworth illegally every week for France, along with guns, powder, cloth, grain and foodstuffs. Local fishermen found it worthwhile to hang around the beach in the hope of making some easy money.

Lulworth was also popular among pirates, whose vessels often sought shelter in the cove knowing they were unlikely to be disturbed. In the 16th century much of the booty brought ashore here was carted after dark to Bryanston Manor, near Blandford, home of Sir Richard Rogers. There were vast sums to be made from piracy – an attack on a single convoy of ships could yield a haul worth £10,000!

When smuggling began to take off early in the 18th century, Lulworth was well placed to take advantage. Philip Taylor, who was Collector of Customs at Weymouth around 1720, described it as the most notorious smuggling centre on his entire section of coast. In his reports to London, he wrote of smugglers operating "in such great numbers, armed and disguised, that the officers, if they meet them, can't possibly oppose them therein, nor do otherwise than search for the goods in suspected places".

The Lulworth smugglers had some useful allies. Long-serving Customs boatman John Gregory was related to many of the local fishermen and friendly with the rest and his son was "frequently called out of his dwelling house by the smugglers". Riding officer Philip Newton's connections were equally dubious. In 20 years at Lulworth he had inevitably "contracted a very intimate acquaintance with all the smugglers of the place".

Both Gregory and Newton were accused by an East Lulworth farmer of "conniving at the running of goods and corresponding with known smugglers and other indirect practices". Newton was said to have taken bribes and even to have helped smugglers unload and sell their goods; both he and Gregory were accused of commissioning smugglers to bring them brandy from France.

Even the landowning Weld family of Lulworth Castle came under suspicion. In April 1719 Philip Taylor ordered his men to search the castle and "several other suspected houses in East and West Lulworth". They left the castle empty-handed but found four gallons of brandy and 12 pounds of pepper at the home of Edward Bagwell, a tenant on the Weld Estate. Such discoveries were more the exception than the rule. With public sympathy on the smugglers' side, it was not surprising that searches "very often proves ineffectual and expensive to the officers", as Taylor put it.

Many smugglers were so ruthless that Customs officers who took them on were putting their lives at risk. One group of officers, who challenged 10 or 11 smugglers as they headed inland from Lulworth Cove at 3 o'clock in the morning, was attacked with swords, flails and clubs. The officers managed to get their hands on several casks of brandy and wine but most were regained by the smugglers and one was deliberately staved, spilling an anker (eight and a half gallons) of wine. (Staving was a tactic smugglers sometimes used to deprive officers of the substantial rewards they could claim on seized goods.)

The incident turned into a running battle which continued for 12 hours! Eventually the smugglers disappeared into a coppice at Owermoigne, not to be seen again. The area was searched but only four abandoned anker casks were found. "The rest," reported Taylor, "was carried off from the smugglers by the country people of three or four parishes adjacent who, being alarmed at our encounter, fell into the wood before we could possibly get thither."

A leading Dorset smuggler in the 1720s was Charles Weeks, whose cargoes included coffee, pepper, spices and Venezuelan cocoa beans. His ships were unloaded in Lulworth Cove and the goods carried to the village of Winfrith for storage in cottages, barns and outhouses. Later they would be loaded on to carts and wagons and transported to London, which was the only market for such exotic commodities.

A century later, when the formation of the Coastguard and other changes forced smugglers to be more devious and secretive than they were in the 1700s, women at Lulworth carried smuggled spirits in small tubs hidden in linen baskets piled high with clothes or in animal bladders concealed beneath their voluminous petticoats. If approached by an officer, they would stand around gossiping, arms folded, until he had gone.

Between 1827 and 1844, the records of Dorchester Jail list ten smugglers from East or West Lulworth, two of them on charges involving firearms. They included labourer James Davis, who served four months for smuggling in 1830 and was back within two years charged with assisting in the landing of contraband goods, being armed with offensive weapons and assaulting Customs officers. On this occasion he was acquitted.

As the firearms charges suggest, many smugglers were prepared to go to great lengths to defend their goods. Inevitably, this led to occasional tragedies. In 1832 two Lulworth Coastguards patrolling the clifftops at Lulworth were attacked by smugglers armed with "swingles", a form of flail. Both were "beaten unmercifully" by the smugglers. One of the officers, Boatman Duke, was left for dead but recovered; the other, Lulworth's chief officer Lieutenant Thomas Knight, was dragged to the edge of the cliff and thrown to his death. It was his 42nd birthday.

The Walk: Leave the car park and turn right towards the sea. The route passes the Information Centre, millpond and several shops and hotels.

At the end of the road take the steps to the right, which lead to the top of the cliff, where you will have a fine view over the famous Cove, formed within an almost perfect circle of rock. In the other direction is a view across to Portland.

There is a telescope at the lookout point, and good views over Stair Hole, where the movement which made these cliffs was so strong that the strata are vertical. The rocks here are more than 150 million years old, which makes them older than the Alps.

Follow the path across the cliff and back to the car park. At the far end is a stile and a signpost pointing to Durdle Door. Once over the stile, follow the path which leads up the cliff. It is easy to see from a distance, as it shows white against the grass.

At the top there is a marvellous view of the bay, and eastwards along the cliffs to St Aldhelm's (or Alban's) Head.

At the time of writing the path was diverted slightly because of severe erosion. The route is clearly marked with yellow waymarkers.

If you look back you will be able to see as far as Bournemouth on a clear day. The Purbeck Hills stretch away to the east, with a wide band of contrasting lush farmland in their shelter.

As the path crests the rise, Portland comes into view, also the folded cliffs ahead. This is a very dramatic stretch of coast, with a stack and arch visible in the distance, where the softer rock has been eroded by the sea.

Cross the double stile and go down the path to the milestone.

You will soon come to the top of the cliff at Durdle Door. This famous arch is featured in all the guide books, and justifiably so. It is a stunning natural fea-

The Beach at Lulworth Cove

ture. There are steps down to the beach.

Carry on along the path, which rises up the next slope to provide an excellent view over the arch and twisted strata.

The path leads over the top of the rise and down, giving a closer view of the stack and arch. Ahead you will see a vertical-looking path. But don't worry – you don't have to climb it!

At the bottom of the slope turn right at the milestone, following the arrow marked Campsite/Newlands Farm. Climb the stile, which has a special gate for dogs.

Follow the pleasant grassy path along the valley. There is a fence on the left, and the whole area is sheltered and peaceful.

The path curves to the right and passes through a gate and stile marked with a yellow arrow – a spot blessed with the intriguing name of Scratchy Bottom!

Walk up the slope, across the grass to a gate and stile. Go through, and you will see a caravan site to the right.

Cross the grass diagonally to the left, in the direction indicated by the yellow arrow, until you reach a gate and signpost in the far corner of the field.

Go through the gate and turn right, following the sign to Newlands Farm.

At the junction with the metalled road (Newlands Farm Cottage is opposite), turn right, walk until you come to another junction, and then turn right again.

You are now on the service road to the caravan park. There is a grassy footpath beside the road.

Follow the path into the Durdle Door Caravan Park and walk through the site.

As you leave the campsite there is a signpost on the left. Cross the stile beside it and follow the sign to West Lulworth.

The path runs along the edge of the

Stair Hole, Lulworth

field with a fence on the left.

Climb the stile into the next field, where you will be able to see the Winfrith-Lulworth road to the left.

After crossing another stile the path leads down a slope to a stile and signpost.

Ignore the stile and follow the sign to Lulworth Cove and car park.

The path skirts the hill and gives good views over the village before bringing you back to the stile at the edge of the car park.

Walk No: 14 THE BATTLE OF HOOKS WOOD
Farnham and Chettle

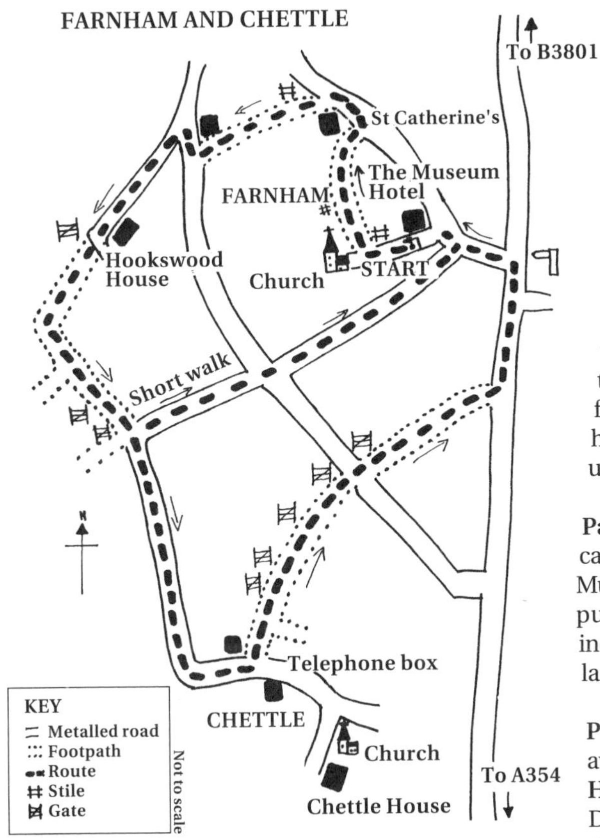

Distance: Longer walk approx 7 kms (4.4 miles); shorter walk approx 4 kms (2.5 miles).

Maps: OS Landranger 184 Salisbury and the Plain and 195 Bournemouth, Purbeck and surrounding area. Map ref: ST 957 151.

Degree of difficulty: This is a pleasant, easy walk through lush countryside and farmland. The views are pleasant and far reaching on a clear day. There are only three stiles and no steep hills.

How to get there: Follow the A354 Blandford to Salisbury road beyond Tarrant Hinton and take one of the next three left-hand turnings (the first leads through Chettle). Then follow the signs to Farnham and find the Museum Hotel.

Parking: There is a free car park for patrons of the Museum Hotel and some public parking nearby, including a strip of public land opposite the pub.

Pub facilities: The award-winning **Museum Hotel,** which has held the Dorset Pub of the Year title among others, dates back to Cromwellian times and was formerly the Old Ash Inn. It was renamed at the turn of the century after the world-famous museum, opened at Farnham in the 1890s by the father of modern archaeology, General Pitt-Rivers, who lived nearby. The museum attracted 12,000 visitors in 1899 alone and the pub was extended to meet the demand for refreshments and accommodation in the village. The museum itself closed some years ago and enthusiasts would have to travel to Salisbury or Oxford to see some of Pitt-Rivers' vast collections. But the Museum Hotel lives on as a popular free house with four hotel bedrooms in a converted stable block.

The Museum has a candlelit dining room and two bars, one with an inglenook fireplace and original bread oven, the other with a selection of pub games. There is also a beer garden with a real tractor for children to play on. Children will be served only in the conservatory and dining room.

The Museum's impressive selection of traditional pub food is always available and attracts customers from many miles around. Real ale is served. Opening times: 11 am-3 pm and 6-11 pm Monday-Saturday, 12 noon-3 pm and 7-10.30 pm Sunday. Tel: 01725 516261.

Other attractions: Chettle House is an early 17th century building with strong smuggling traditions and, reputedly, a secret underground passage. Open 11 am-5 pm daily except Tuesday and Saturday. Gardens open Good Friday to the second Sunday in October except Tuesday and Saturday. Tel: 01258 830209.

The Larmer Tree Gardens at Tollard Royal take their name from a wych elm known to have existed in the tenth century, which became a landmark indicating parish and county boundaries and a meeting place for, among others, King John's henchmen when he was hunting in the royal forest of Cranborne Chase. The present larmer tree is an oak. The Victorian pleasure gardens were developed by General Pitt-Rivers towards the end of the 19th century and include exotic structures such as the Roman Temple, Victorian Singing Theatre and the General's Indian Room from where he watched musical and theatrical performances. The gardens are now the venue for an annual music festival and other events and since 1995 have been open to the public on Thursdays, Sundays and bank holidays in spring and summer. To check the latest opening times, dates, etc, tel: 01725 516228.

History: This walk covers a small part of the ancient royal hunting forest of Cranborne Chase, where kings and nobles came for sport over many centuries. Until the 19th century, the interests of deer were second only to the interests of those who came to hunt them. A shared interest of hunter and hunted was the preservation of Cranborne Chase as a wilderness and it remained a "rough and mysterious country" for hundreds of years. Being such wild country, it was also a refuge for poachers, fugitives and criminals, including smugglers, who lived here and stopped here with their contraband on the way inland from the coast.

At Hooks Wood, near Farnham, there was a famous battle between smugglers and dragoons in March 1779, which was vividly described in a newspaper:

"The Excise officer at Cranborne, having intelligence of upwards of 20 horses, loaded with smuggled goods, passing by that place, he with six dragoons, quartered in Cranborne, armed with guns, swords, pistols, etc, went in pursuit of them and, about 4 o'clock in the afternoon, finding the goods in a coppice near Hooks Wood in the parish of Farnham, they immediately seized them, loaded their horses and began to carry them away; upon which the smugglers, who were not far distant, collected themselves to the number of 40 or 50 and attacked the dragoons in order to rescue

The Museum Hotel, Farnham

their goods, when a desperate fray ensued.

"The soldiers with their broad swords behaved with great resolution and bravery. The Exciseman, it is said, fired his fusee and wounded one of the smugglers in the arm, so that it must be amputated. Another smuggler was shot in the left breast, and the ball went through him. The smugglers made use of large clubs and, being highly exasperated, dealt their blows about very severely. They were at last victorious. They beat the soldiers in an inhuman manner, broke their swords, demolished their firearms and carried off their horses in triumph, but they [the horses] have all since been found."

During the night word reached the authorities that two of the smugglers were sleeping at an inn on the Blandford road and next morning the pair were arrested by another party of dragoons from Wimborne and committed to the county jail at Dorchester. They were subsequently tried at the Dorset Assizes for "taking goods from some officers of Excise" but were both acquitted. A third smuggler died of the wounds he sustained in the battle of Hooks Wood. But the remainder of the 40 or 50 involved were never identified and remained at large.

It is tempting to think that the pub where the two captured smugglers were arrested was the old Blacksmith's Arms on the Blandford to Salisbury road at Thorney Down, two or three miles from Farnham. The pub was certainly a regular haunt of smugglers and a year or two before the Hooks Wood incident was kept by none other than Isaac Gulliver, the most famous smuggler in Dorset history. A few years before that the licensee was Gulliver's father-in-law, William Beale. When Gulliver took over he changed the pub's name to the King's

An unusual attraction in the grounds of the Museum Hotel

Arms. Later still it became the Thorney Down Inn. The building survives as a private house and to this day has peepholes in its doors enabling someone at the back of the house to see right through to the front.

The village of Chettle, which features in the longer route, is another place with smuggling associations and Chettle House is today owned by a descendant of Isaac Gulliver, Mr Patrick Bourke. The house is supposed to have a secret underground passage of the kind frequently used by smugglers, though Mr Bourke is unable to confirm the truth of this or otherwise. Chettle House was built for the Chafin family in 1711 and in the late 18th century was the home of the Rev William Chafin, a friend of Gulliver and the man who sold him the prehistoric hillfort of Eggardon, west of Dorchester, where the smuggler planted a clump of trees as a landmark for his ships. The plantation was cut down by government order.

The Walk: Turn right out of the pub car park and walk along the lane. Opposite the old carved well, turn right along the path which goes past the church. At the end of the path is a stile with two yellow arrows.

Climb over the stile and walk along the right hand edge of the field. Halfway across are a stile and a footpath on the right. The path would be easy to miss but there is an electricity pole opposite.

Keep to the right edge of this field until you come to a farmyard. Turn right towards the village street, where you come out opposite Eton Cottage.

Turn left and after a few yards pass a converted chapel called St Catherine's, built in 1865. The path lies to the side of this house. Once over the stile, cross the field. The exit lies at the far right hand corner of the field, next to the building. The official footpath crosses the field to the side of the middle electricity pole which lies directly ahead — but walkers are asked to skirt the edge if necessary.

Leave the field and turn right along the road. After a few yards turn left into a narrow metalled lane. There is a pretty view here and to the right lies Hooks Wood, scene of the bloody battle between smugglers and soldiers in 1779.

The lane is quiet and leads past Hookswood House (called Hookswood Farm on the map). The path passes between trees and a fence before coming to a gate barring the way. It is marked with a blue arrow. After going through the gate (and leaving it closed behind you) turn right along the edge of the field.

About halfway between your point of entry to the field and the wood ahead of you, turn left and cross the field, following the blue bridleway sign. At the time of writing the farmer had left an unploughed strip of grass.

Go straight across the field, which at the time of our walk was laid to linseed. The misty blue sea of linseed was ablaze with poppies, creating a scene reminiscent of an Impressionist painting.

At the gate beside the pile of discarded flints (a temporary landmark which may or may not outlive sales of this book!), walk straight on, along the wide grassy track. You will come to another gate which leads to a road.

For the ***shorter walk***, turn left and keep straight on at the cross roads to return to the Museum Hotel.

For the ***longer walk,*** go straight on. The road passes between tall trees and soon reaches the outskirts of Chettle. The road bears to the left.

Look for the flint track on the left, marked with a blue arrow on a signpost. Just past it is a telephone box on the right. This is the next stage of our walk but you may wish to go straight on to visit the small but attractive Chettle church or Chettle House.

To continue (or resume) the longer walk, take the flint track referred to in the previous paragraph. Where it bears to the right, go straight along the grassy footpath. It passes between hedges and then opens out on to the edge of a field. At the top of the rise go through two gates into the next field.

Rev William Chafin

Walk along the right side of this field. The gentle climb will give you a good view over the surrounding rolling countryside. Go through a single metal gate and cross the next field. The next gate takes you to a road.

Turn right on to the road, then almost immediately left through the metal gate with the blue arrow. Walk along the edge of this field for more excellent views over woods and farms.

Go through the gate and turn left on to the road. Walk downhill to Minchington Farm, just after which is a signpost pointing to Farnham.

Turn left and you will soon be back at the pub

THE SMUGGLERS' INN
Osmington Mills and Ringstead

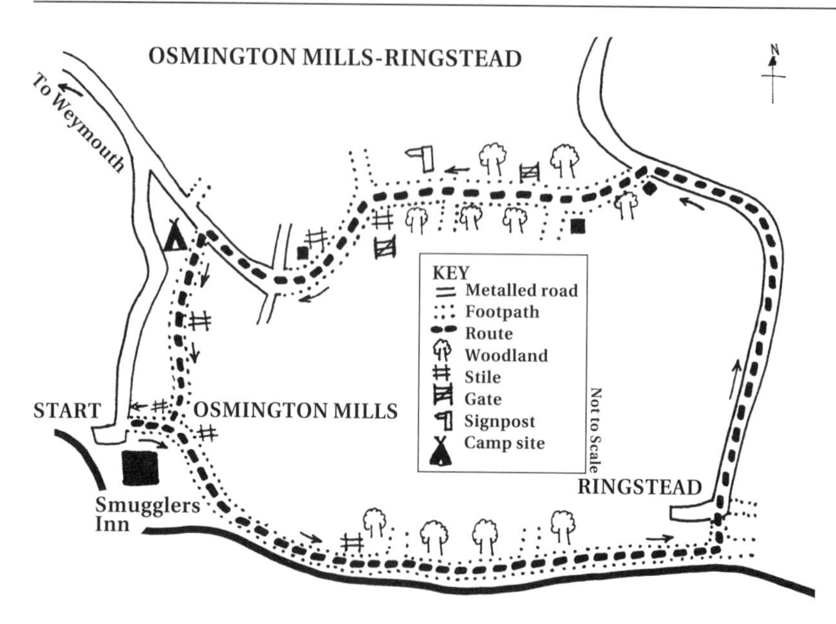

Distance: 4.5 kms (2.8 miles)

Maps: OS Landranger 194 Dorchester, Weymouth and surrounding area. Map ref: SY 735 817.

Degree of difficulty: This is a well-signposted walk. There are some stiles but they are low. The cliff sections are relatively safe as the edge is screened by wire or bushes.

How to get there: From the A353 Weymouth to Warmwell road, turn south at Osmington (four miles north-east of Weymouth) and follow the lane to Osmington Mills.

Parking: The Smugglers Inn has a large clifftop car park and an eminently sensible arrangement for people who wish to use it. The car park is particularly well used in summer but walkers may still use it on payment of a parking fee (£2 at the time of writing). Those who also choose to use the pub can use the parking ticket towards purchases over the bar. There is also some roadside parking.

Pub facilities: The Smugglers Inn is an old and attractive part-thatched building, allegedly dating from the 13th century and with genuine smuggling traditions. Inside it has more than its share of timber beams and columns and an amazing array of nooks and crannies. It is a free house offering a wide range of drinks including real ales and an impressive selection of bar meals, set menu and full a la carte. Daily fresh fish and lobster are specialities and the wine

The Smugglers' Inn, Osmington Mills

list offers 40 choices.

The Smugglers Inn — known to locals as "the Smuggs" — sits neatly in a hollow beside a stream and has plenty of sheltered picnic benches in the garden as well as swings and a slide for the children. Opening times: Summer 11 am-11 pm Monday-Saturday, 12 noon-11 pm Sunday; winter 11 am-3 pm and 6-11 pm Monday-Saturday, 12 noon-3 pm and 7-10.30 pm Sunday. Tel: 01305 833125.

History: The relatively remote seaside location of Osmington Mills ensured its place in the smuggling trade and many a group of smugglers whiled away a merry evening in the ancient Smugglers Inn, which in their day was called the Crown and, more recently, the Picnic. Nearby Ringstead was also a popular landing place for contraband. At the Smugglers Inn glass bottles cemented into the walls just below the eaves (but now obscured from view) are said to have been a secret sign that this was a "safe house", where smugglers could find helpers sympathetic to the cause. The famous French smuggler Pierre Latour — known locally as French Peter — is said to have had his headquarters here. Another famous visitor was the artist John Constable, who spent his honeymoon at Osmington and painted his famous view of Weymouth Bay from the beach.

In one part of the inn is an old fireplace which the smugglers used to sit around discussing past adventures and planning others for the future. Tradition has it that on one summer's evening, a particularly keen young Preventive officer hid up the chimney hoping to eavesdrop on the smugglers' conversation and gain some clue to their plans. It was no coincidence that, although it was summer, the smugglers felt the cold that evening and insisted that the landlord light a fire. Before long the smoke got too much for the poor officer, who fell into the fireplace to be humiliatingly stripped of his uniform and sent home "dressed only in soot".

Another story — but a tragic one — was told in the early 1950s by retired fisherman Arthur Toms, whose clifftop home at Osmington Mills was built around an old gun emplacement. According to Mr Toms, his grandfather was a smuggler with a price on his head, to be paid if he was taken dead or alive. One day the grandfather's brother-in-law arrived for a few days holiday. Unfortunately he was mistaken for the smuggler and shot dead by a Preventive officer while tending his relatives' garden.

One of Osmington's most active smugglers 200 years ago was a fisherman called William Waters or Walters. The records of Dorchester Prison reveal that he was caught at least five times between 1791 and 1827 — more than any other known smuggler in Dorset history. Four other Osmington smugglers also appear in the gaol lists, including James Champ, who did six months in 1821 and six months hard labour in both 1835 and 1838, and young Joseph Waters, a 15-year-old with "a great impediment in his speech", who was accused of smuggling in 1819 but acquitted.

The Charles family was also heavily involved in Osmington's smuggling ventures. John Charles appeared in the dock alongside William Waters in 1791, charged with assaulting and obstructing Customs officers. And in the 1820s Emmanuel Charles of Osmington was one of the biggest names in Dorset smuggling circles, controlling a gang which had a reputation for ruthlessly attacking officers of the newly-formed Coastguard.

Emmanuel Charles dealt mainly in contraband spirits which Customs officials described as "so raw and unpalatable as to be totally unfit for consumption". It fact, the stuff was so rough that it had to undergo "a process of rectification" in illegal stills which existed only in large towns and cities in distant parts of the country. Amazingly, most of it travelled inland on stage coaches which were then the main form of public transport. The tubs of spirits were packed into standard packing cases indistinguishable from those used for legitimate goods, thus minimising the risk of discovery.

According to Poole's Customs collector, the Charles gang were "more or less concerned in every illicit transaction" in south and east Dorset in the late 1820s. But another report suggests that they had gone out of business by about 1830. An important factor in this sudden decline in fortunes was the seizure of Emmanuel Charles' ship The Integrity, which masqueraded as a fishing vessel but in reality was "exclusively employed in smuggling and has been so for years". Emmanuel's son Richard Charles was on board at the time of capture along with crewman William Cockram. Both were sentenced to serve in His Majesty's Navy (not an attractive prospect in those days) but Cockram was found unfit for service and sent to prison instead. Emmanuel Charles tried to persuade the authorities that his son was also unfit due to a "consumptive habit of body and decaying constitution". But after two medicals, doctors and officers concluded that young Richard was as "fit and able" as any man ever enlisted in similar circumstances.

The Walk: As you face the Smugglers Inn there is a footpath immediately to the left of the building. Walk to its end and climb the stile, which has a yellow arrow on it.

The path goes up a slope via a stile to the cliff, where there are fine views to Weymouth, Portland and the Chesil Beach. There is a very wide horizon with the opportunity to watch all sorts of shipping.

The grassy track goes between bushes and emerges on the cliff.

There is a view ahead to Ringstead Bay and its far headland White Nothe. In certain conditions hang gliders can be seen soaring over the downs to the north.

After the next stile the track goes straight on, passing between more bushes, with glimpses of the sea.

Go into the wood and follow the yellow arrow down the steps. At the bottom cross the plank over a stream and climb the steps on the other side.

Walk through the woods and after crossing three more planks the path opens out on to a grassy area with cottages on the left. This is Ringstead, where countless illicit cargoes came ashore a couple of centuries ago.

Go straight on past the houses, following the path. Take the gravel path to the left which leads inland.

It becomes a metalled road and passes the Ringstead kiosk and car park.

To the right are excellent views of the cliffs with the occasional cottage perched amongst them.

As the road turns the corner you are looking west again towards Portland. Just past a house called Spinney Brook, at the edge of the woods, take the gravel footpath on the left. There is a yellow arrow on the fence post.

Soon after passing a bungalow, the track forks. Bear right, following the yellow arrow. Go through the gate and continue through the woods. This is easy walking, made all the more pleasant by the sound of the sea in the distance.

When you reach two yellow arrows and a signpost, go straight on towards Osmington Mills. Ignore the next signpost, which points to the coastal path, and walk straight on to the stile next to a metal gate.

Once over the stile, turn left; follow the signpost arm which points to Osmington Mills. Cross the plank bridge and follow the rutted track. Head towards the cottages which you will see ahead of you in the distance.

As you approach the thatched cottage you will see a stile in front of it, in the corner of the field. Climb the stile, then turn right towards Osmington, following the sign high up on the telegraph pole opposite.

The grassy track leads to a metalled road. Bear right down the hill. All other tracks are marked "Private road".

e passes between hedges, giving good views to Weymouth and Portland.

Just past the water purification works look out for the yellow arrow on the left. It is on a fence post and the path leads straight across a campsite.

Climb the stile, marked with a yellow arrow, and cross the field, following the track.

Just past the house on the right, climb the stile on the same side and head back to the pub.

'SPIRITS FROM THE DEEP ARISE!'
Bournemouth

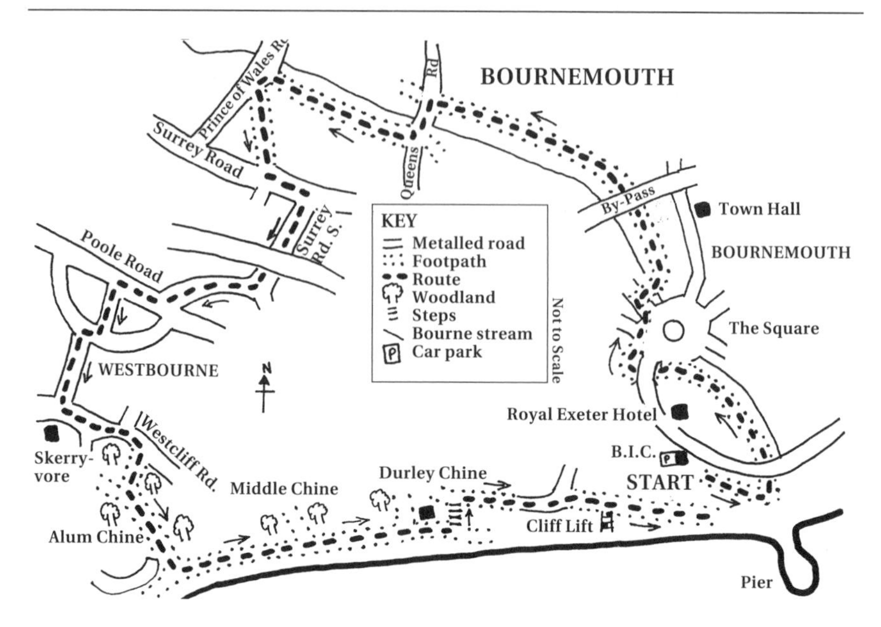

Distance: 6 kms (3.75 miles)

Maps: Bournemouth Street Plan (Estate Publications Red Book) is the most useful for this walk. See page 38.

Also, OS Landranger 195 Bournemouth, Purbeck and surrounding area.

Map ref: SZ 087 908.

Degree of difficulty: There is one flight of steps leading from the beach to the cliff top. Apart from this the walk is very easy — no stiles, no gates, no mud!

How to get there: On reaching Bournemouth, follow the signs to the town centre. The car park and Royal Exeter Hotel are both in Exeter Road, best reached (due to recent pedestrianisation schemes) from the Lansdowne, Bath Road and the Pier Approach fly over.

Parking: The Royal Exeter has a car park but parking there is strictly controlled with the threat of wheel clamps for those without receipts. Walkers intending to use the hotel may use the car park providing they give their vehicle registration number to the receptionist beforehand. Alternatively there are many pay-for public car parks within walking distance, such as the Bournemouth International Centre multi-storey opposite, which has 700 spaces.

Pub facilities: The Royal Exeter Hotel is the most historic building in central Bournemouth and the only one dating back to the time when Bournemouth beach was a favourite landing place of smugglers. The oldest part of the building — which today includes the Tre-

Tregonwell's seaside mansion, now part of the Royal Exeter Hotel

gonwell Bar — was built in 1810 as a seaside mansion for a local squire, Captain Lewis Tregonwell, and his wife, Henrietta. Tregonwell — still known as the "Founder of Bournemouth" — has himself been linked to smuggling (see History section). The hotel acquired its "Royal" prefix from a visit by Elizabeth of Prussia in 1888.

The Royal Exeter is a two-star hotel with 45 rooms plus the Dorset Suite with its four-poster bed and spa bath. Facilities include two bars, a large restaurant and a conference suite and there is live entertainment in the Tregonwell Bar in summer. Real ales are served in the upstairs Exeter Bar, which is open all day throughout the year. There is a comprehensive menu of restaurant meals and bar snacks.

Opening times: The Royal Exeter is open 24 hours a day throughout the year. Breakfasts are served from 7.30-9.30 am Monday-Friday and 8-10 am at weekends. Restaurant meals and bar snacks are available from 12 noon-2.30 pm and 5.30-10.30 pm (11 pm Saturdays) in July and August, 12 noon-2 pm and 6-9.30 pm (10 pm Saturdays) during the rest of the year. Tel: 01202 290566.

Other eating and drinking establishments in central Bournemouth are too numerous to mention.

Optional extras: Swimming costume; bucket and spade.

Other attractions: This walk in relatively urban Bournemouth offers a range of things to do or look at and walkers may wish to allocate more time than the distance would suggest.

The route passes the beach and Pier with all their attractions. In the summer season there are cafes and kiosks along the seafront as well as deckchairs and seats for those who wish to pause awhile to enjoy beach life.

You will also walk along the clifftops, with their fine views of the bay, the Purbeck Hills and the Isle of Wight, and pass one of Bournemouth's famous cliff lifts. If you have children, allow time for a return ride. They will also enjoy the playground rides at Westbourne.

Swimmers have the chance to bathe in the sea or in the Bournemouth International Centre's leisure pool with wave machine. Gardeners will find much of interest in the Upper and Lower Gardens with their seasonal displays and many unusual trees.

You will also go through the Westbourne Arcade, built in the 1880s, pass the site of Skerryvore, where Robert Louis Stevenson lived and wrote for two of his most productive years, and walk the length of one of the chines, as the breaks in the cliffs are known.

History: Walking around Bournemouth today, it is hard to imagine this modern seaside resort and conference town as it was two centuries ago. Until the early 19th century, it consisted of little more than wild, uninhabited heathland between the ancient towns at Poole, Wimborne and Christchurch, the villages of Kinson, Holdenhurst and Throop and the sea. It was known as Bourne Heath and attracted few visitors apart from turf-cutters and smugglers.

A vivid description of Bourne Heath was written by the Duke of Rutland after he passed through with a companion in 1795. "From Christchurch," he wrote, "we proceeded on horseback towards Poole. After going about two miles on the highroad, we turned off by the advice of a farmer, who told us we should find a much shorter way by going to the left, which however would not do for a carriage. We accordingly followed his direction till we came to the top of a high cliff, where we could not find the least track of a road. We were however in some degree recompensed by a most delightful view of the sea.

"After enjoying this noble scene, we turned our horses' heads in order to discover some road, which we at last effected. We rode as we thought in the direction towards Poole, for on the barren uncultivated heath where we were, there was not a human being to direct us. We were not however mistaken, as after a most dreary ride we found ourselves on the high road, from whence we looked down upon Poole and its environs."

The combination of deserted wilderness and gently sloping beaches made Bourne Heath especially attractive to smugglers. Down the decades countless cargoes were landed along the seven-mile shore between Sandbanks and Hengistbury Head. The goods would then be loaded on to horses and wagons and carried inland by way of the chines or at Bourne Bottom, site of the modern town centre and Pier Approach. Several of present-day Bournemouth's artery roads — such as Wimborne Road, Christchurch Road and Holdenhurst Road — are said to have originated as smugglers' tracks.

In the 18th century there was only one house in what is now central Bournemouth. It stood close to the site of today's Square and was known as the Decoy Pond House, though its purpose had at least as much to do with smug-

The Royal Exeter Hotel

gling as it did with wildfowling and decoy ducks. In 1762 the house became a temporary prison for a man called Joseph Manuel, who was kidnapped from his home at nearby Iford by smugglers who suspected him of being an informer. Manuel was later shipped to the channel island of Alderney and left there to make his own way home.

In 1771 the Decoy Pond House was named in Customs documents as the home of William Harris, brother-in-law and professional associate of Edward Beake, one of Bourne Heath's most notorious smugglers. Beake was the organiser of many successful landings on Bournemouth beach. Once, after seeing his wagon and 60 tubs seized on the heath, he used force to recapture them. The Customs riding officers gave chase and shot one of the smugglers' horses "notwithstanding which they got clear off, the smugglers confining the officers to prevent their pursuing the wagon near two hours". Beake became one of the area's most wanted men and one of the cheekiest. He once secured his release from arrest by handing over £40 to the arresting officer, then sued the bewildered official for compensation on the grounds that he had exceeded his authority in accepting it.

Another of Bourne's most active smugglers was the great Isaac Gulliver, whose base for some years was Kinson, one of the villages on the edge of the heath. According to a story first published as long ago as the 1850s — just 30 years after Gulliver's death — his last run took place at Bourne around 1800 and was a fittingly grand occasion. It is said there were three luggers anchored in Poole Bay, each heavily laden with contraband; that the convoy of horses and wagons used to carry the cargo inland stretched two miles across Bourne Heath; and that the grand procession was led by Gulliver himself, suitably mounted on a white steed.

Kinson is also the burial place of the Wiltshire smuggler Robert Trotman, shot dead in 1765 in a skirmish with the Royal Navy during a landing on the beach between Sandbanks and Bournemouth (see Kinson-Longham walk). The incident is the most famous of many that occurred on the golden sands which, within a few decades, were

The 'founder of Bournemouth', Captain Lewis Tregonwell

attracting the first of the millions of holidaymakers.

A vivid picture of smuggling operations on Bourne Heath was given in a Customs report in 1804 which estimated that between Sandbanks and Hengistbury Head 80,000 gallons (363,000 litres) of spirits were illegally landed each year. The report names the main landing spots as North Haven Point (Sandbanks), the Head (Flag Head, Canford Cliffs), Alum Chine, Bourne Mouth and Boscombe. It adds that the goods "are mostly conveyed in wagons and carts into the interior, where they are deposited in caves or concealed in the woods and other secret places, more particularly the New Forest, which are seldom to be found, and from thence they are occasionally conveyed, principally on horses' backs, and disposed of throughout the counties of Hants and Wilts".

A favourite haunt of smugglers at this time was central Bournemouth's first pub, the Tapps Arms (later the Tregonwell Arms), which stood for most of the 19th century at the corner of Christchurch Road and Post Office Road, within a stone's throw of the Square. The inn — demolished in 1885 — took its later name from Captain Lewis Tregonwell, who built the first seaside mansion at Bourne and earned himself the title of "founder of Bournemouth". The building — begun in 1810 after Tregonwell's wife visited the spot and fell in love with it — today survives as part of the Royal Exeter Hotel.

It has been suggested that Tregonwell himself was in league with the smugglers. The evidence is thin and highly circumstantial, although he would certainly have been aware of the smugglers as commander of the Dorset Rangers who patrolled the beach and clifftops here when a French invasion was feared between 1796 and 1802. The suggestion of a direct link with smuggling was raised following the discovery in 1930 of an underground chamber beneath Portman Lodge, the cottage of Tregonwell's butler, which stood a short distance from the Royal Exeter. The arched chamber — ten feet long, seven feet wide and six feet high — was three feet below ground level and its entrance was a trap door. Was it really a hiding place for contraband newly-landed on the beach?

We will probably never know the answer to that but there is some evidence that smuggling continued into the early years of Bournemouth's career as a holiday resort. It appears in an unpublished play, written in 1815 by Mrs Richard Drax Grosvenor, who had a cottage on the West Cliff. The play is set 60 years into the future and portrays an image of Bournemouth in 1812 as "a lonely and desolate spot" where "the only neighbours were a gang of gipsies and smugglers". Mrs Grosvenor's cartoon illustrations feature members of the Tregonwell family and a smuggling scene. Beneath a drawing of casks on the beach is the "Bournists' Motto" — "Spirits from the Deep Arise! Oh! Arise!"

The Walk: From the Royal Exeter Hotel, turn left and walk to the Pier, which offers its own little circular route (up one side and back the other!) for those who wish to make a short detour. In summer pleasure boats leave from here, including the paddle steamer Waverley, which visits in September.

Opposite the Pier is the entrance to the Lower Gardens. Take the main path (to the left of the Bourne Stream) and walk right through, keeping the crazy golf on your left and the bandstand on your right. The flower beds are always full of seasonal displays and in summer there are special candle lighting evenings as part of the illuminations.

At the end of the gardens, go through the underpass and turn right to emerge on the pavement outside Debenhams in Bournemouth Square. As you survey the hive of urban activity around you, it is interesting to consider that had you stood on the same spot 200 years ago there would have been just one building in view — the Decoy Pond House, which stood almost on the site of the present-day Square and was a popular resort of 18th century smugglers.

Walk a little further to cross the road by the pedestrian crossing near Boots the Chemist.

Go down the steps into the Upper Gardens and under the pergola.

Turn left at the end of this path and keep the Bourne Stream on your left. Pass the War Memorial, also on the left.

As you walk further up the gardens, you are will encounter more natural vegetation and probably fewer people. There are also some unusual trees, which help to make this an attractive area to walk through at any time of the year.

Keep to the right of the tennis courts and walk under the town centre by-pass, following the sign to Coy Pond. The stream is still on your left.

When the path comes out on to a road, turn left and walk a few yards along the pavement before crossing over and going into the next part of the gardens. The Bourne Stream is now on your right.

This part is particularly pretty in autumn, when the trees are ablaze with colour. A little further on is a tiny water tower built in brick in the style of a fairy-tale castle complete with turret.

At the end of this section of the gardens, turn left on to the pavement, and immediately left again, into a narrow footpath running between the bushes. It is not marked on the street map.

At the end of the footpath turn left into Surrey Road, then take the second on the right, which is Surrey Road South. At the end of this road follow the sign to "Westbourne via subway". The path first goes under a Victorian brick railway arch, then contrastingly through a modern square subway under the Wessex Way road.

Follow the road into Westbourne Close. There is a children's playground on the right.

At the end of Westbourne Close turn left to the main road and then right to the centre of Westbourne. There are many interesting shops and delicatessens here.

Cross the road at the pelican crossing and walk through the Westbourne Arcade, built in the early 1880s by local property developer Henry Joy, whose other projects included the highly successful Bournemouth Arcade in the town centre.

At the far end of the Westbourne Arcade, cross the road and turn right. Take the first left into R.L. Stevenson Avenue and walk the whole length of the road.

At the end of R.L. Stevenson Avenue is West Cliff Road and facing you is the site of Skerryvore, where the great Robert Louis himself lived between April 1885 and August 1887 and worked, in his own words, "like a weevil in a biscuit". Products of this period of ill health and intensive labour included the classics Kidnapped and The Strange Case of Dr Jekyll and Mr Hyde. The house was demolished after suffering bomb damage in 1940 but the site is open to the public.

As you leave the Skerryvore garden, turn right and walk on until you come to a sign on the right marked Alum Chine.

Follow the sign, and turn into the path. It is narrow and wooded and leads over a bridge to meet another path. Turn left on to the second path, passing the R L Stevenson plaque, and walk straight along the chine, ignoring the bridge immediately to your left.

Considering its proximity to the town centre, Alum Chine remains surprisingly natural and unspoilt and must have changed little in 200 years. It is not hard to imagine a train of horses and wagons, loaded with contraband and ridden by smugglers, trudging up from the beach to the heathland beyond. Such scenes could be witnessed on many occasions in the past.

The path goes under a suspension bridge and down to the sea front.

Turn left on to the promenade and pass Middle Chine before reaching Durley Chine.

Follow the sign marked "Durley Steps". The path is to one side of the Durley Inn, which serves a range of food and drinks.

At the top of the steps, turn right and walk along the cliff path. It is worth the climb for the views over the whole sweep of the bay, from Hengistbury Head in the east to Shell Bay and Old Harry Rocks in the west. On a clear day the Isle of Wight is visible, although it is said that if you can see it there is rain on the way! You might also see one of the cross Channel ferries entering or leaving Poole Harbour. Weather permitting, Corfe Castle is visible in the Purbecks.

When the path meets a road, follow the pavement as far as the Highcliff Hotel, then walk down the slope towards the pier. On the right is the West Cliff lift – open in season.

The Bournemouth International Centre is on the left. At the bottom of the slope turn left and walk back along Exeter Road to the car.

CLARET FOR THE SQUIRE
Milton Abbas

Distance: 4 kms (2.5 miles)

Maps: OS Landranger 194 Dorchester, Weymouth and surrounding area. Map ref: ST 809 020.

Degree of difficulty: This easy walk, although not long, is packed with interest. It provides a variety of landscapes, from farming upland with far-reaching views to sheltered meadowland beside a stream. It even includes a walk along one of the most famous and picturesque streets in Dorset, and a visit to the beautifully situated Milton Abbey and school.

There are a few stiles, one steep slope, and dogs ***must*** be kept on a lead near the farm.

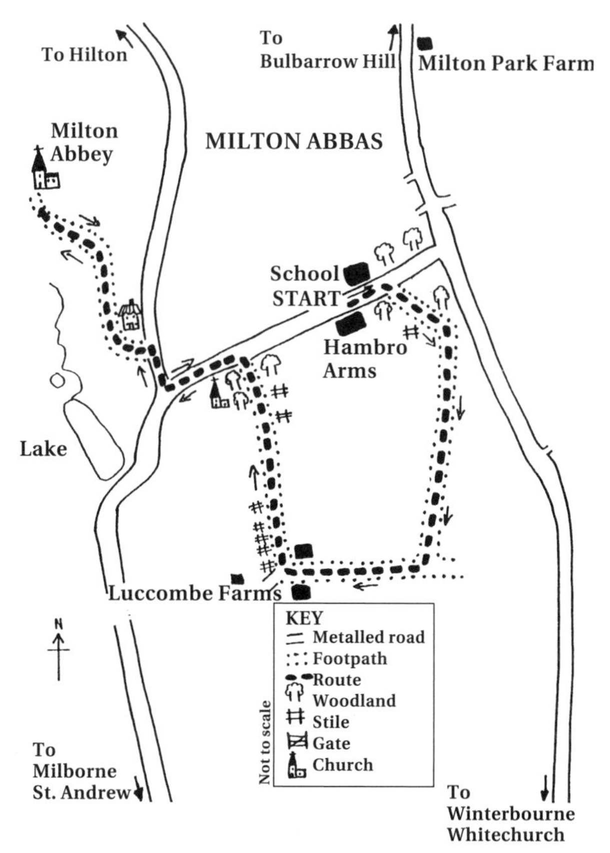

How to get there: From the A354 Puddletown-Blandford road, take one of the turnings signposted Milton Abbas from either Milborne St Andrew or Winterborne Whitechurch. The Hambro Arms is on the main street through the village.

Parking: Walkers using the Hambro Arms are welcome to use the pub car park but there is also ample parking all along the main street of Milton Abbas.

Pub facilities: The Hambro Arms dates from 1760, like most of its neighbours, which were built when an 18th century lord of the manor sought to increase his privacy by demolishing the medieval village close to his house and rebuilding some distance away. In doing so he inadvertently created what is today one of Britain's best-known picture postcard villages.

The thatched Hambro Arms is a cosy and welcoming Greenalls pub where food is a speciality and customers come from miles around. Families are welcomed but not dogs. The menu offers a wide selection of restaurant meals and bar food including a dozen daily specials, children's and vegetarian options and a fine selection of wines. There is also a Sunday carvery, a beer garden and accommodation in the form of two fully en suite rooms, one with a four-poster bed the other twin bedded.

Opening times: Summer 11 am-11 pm Monday-Saturday, 12 noon-10.30 pm Sunday; Winter 11 am-2.30 pm and 7-11 pm Monday-Saturday (Sunday 10.30 pm). Tel: 01258 880233.

Other attractions: Milton Abbey attracts many visitors. At the top of the village is the **Luccombe Farm** fine arts centre. Close by is **Bulbarrow Hill,** the second highest hill in Dorset with spectacular views of the Blackmore Vale and beyond.

History: For obvious reasons, the smugglers of yesteryear kept few written records of their activities and left even fewer for future generations. Two or three autobiographies found their way into print but most contemporary accounts of smugglers and smuggling were penned by Customs officers, court clerks, newspapermen and other outside observers. Local legend provides another source of information and so do the names of certain buildings, paths and tracks. Ferndown has a Smugglers Cottage, Osmington a Smugglers Inn and the name Gulliver attaches itself to several properties associated with the great Dorset smuggler Isaac Gulliver. The parish of Colehill, near Wimborne, has a Smugglers Lane, as does Stourpaine, near Blandford, and Highcliffe, near Christchurch. All provide evidence of some past association with smuggling which was strong enough to pass into general usage.

A further example can be found near Milton Abbas. North of the road between this village and Winterborne Stickland is an old bridleway which runs along the hillside to Turnworth. To locals, it was long known as the Smugglers Path and a glance at a map of the area makes it easy to see why. If we extend the route beyond Turnworth, the next place we come to is Okeford Fitzpaine — a village which, for several decades of the 18th and 19th centuries, was the greatest smuggling centre in North Dorset and the headquarters of the notorious Ridout Gang. A couple of miles north of Okeford Fitzpaine is Fiddleford Mill, where the Ridouts and their helpers stored their contraband (see Fiddleford-Sturminster Newton walk).

The first evidence of Milton Abbas's direct involvement in smuggling comes from the records of Weymouth Custom House, which describe a raid by two Poole Customs officers on no less a place than Milton Abbey House. The date was 1717, when the owner of the house was Sir Jacob Bancks, village squire, MP for Minehead and, ironically, son of the Chief Commissioner of Customs to the King of Sweden. The officers, Scutt and Herring, obviously acting on a tip-off, ascertained that there were two hogsheads or 54-gallon barrels of French claret in Sir Jacob's cellar. The squire's servants were unable to produce any evidence that the import duty had been paid but managed to fob off the officers with a note promising that if they could not produce the certificate next time, the goods would be surrendered.

The Hambro Arms, Milton Abbas

No such certificate ever was produced, of course, and it almost certainly never existed. Yet when the Weymouth Collector of Customs, Philip Taylor, and his men arrived at Milton Abbas a few days later, Sir Jacob complained that he was getting ready to go to church and received them with what Taylor described as "the greatest passion I ever knew". Taylor replied that the smugglers had given him so much trouble lately that he had been to church "but one Sunday for seven weeks past".

After much argument, the officers were eventually admitted to Sir Jacob's wine cellar, where they saw two hogsheads of "extraordinary good claret of a very good growth". Even more interestingly, the barrels were "much sogged with salt water" – a tell-tale sign that they had been imported by smugglers, who used weights and a marker float to sink barrels offshore until they considered it was safe to effect a landing. Taylor attempted to seize the goods as contraband but Sir Jacob flatly refused to let him. Finding themselves outnumbered by the squire's servants and tenants, he decided to give up the attempt and retire gracefully from the scene.

More evidence of Milton Abbas's direct involvement in smuggling appears in the calendar of prisoners at Dorchester Jail. Two smugglers from the parish are listed – 40-year-old labourer James Dunn, of West Milton, who served six months for smuggling after failing to pay a £12 fine in 1823, and 18-year-old sawyer Stephen Arnold, who also served six months for smuggling in 1839.

The Walk: Turn right out of the pub and walk up the hill. Once you have passed the school on your left look out for a footpath on the right, marked by a signpost.

Walk up the slope through the woodland, following the yellow arrows on trees, until you reach a wooden stile at the edge of the woods.

One of the quaint thatched cottages which have made Milton Abbas a picture postcard village

Climb the stile and pass the telegraph pole.

The footpath leads diagonally to the left across the field towards a copse containing a building.

Once on the opposite side, walk along the edge of the field, keeping the hedge on your left. There are fine and far-reaching views over farmland and hills.

Follow the footpath until you reach a farm track. If you have a dog it is most important to have it on a lead at this point.

Turn right on to the track and walk past the outbuildings of Luccombe Farms. Walk downhill to the farmhouse.

Just past the farmhouse and a wooden building on the right, climb the unmarked stile and walk up the bank.

Follow the track across three more unmarked stiles.

At the fifth stile you will find a yellow arrow directing you straight across the large field.

As you walk towards the crest of the hill, you are facing the village, but it is completely hidden in its hollow. There is no sign at all that civilization is so close.

Climb the stile at the top of the hill and walk straight on down the grassy slope and cross the wooden stile.

The path goes straight on down a wooded slope and comes out on to the village street alongside the church.

Turn left on to the road and walk down the hill past all the thatched cottages.

At the junction, turn right (signposted Milton Abbey). A short way along, turn left on to the track marked "Public footpath Milton Abbey Church only". It lies to the left of a thatched cottage.

Footpath leading to Milton Abbey

The walk to the abbey is very pretty and epitomises the English countryside at its best — meadows populated by cows and buttercups, a lake with ducks and coots, a chalk stream conspicuously occupied by fish.

There has been a church on the site of Milton Abbey for over a thousand years. It was originally built as a monastery by King Athelstan and became a thriving medieval market town. The old town was systematically demolished and rebuilt on another site by an 18th century squire, Lord Milton (later Earl of Dorchester), in order to improve the amenity of his own home. The move was unpopular with his tenants but without it Milton Abbas would not be the picture postcard village it is today.

When you are ready to leave, retrace your steps to the village, where you will have an excellent view of the two parallel rows of picturesque cottages built by Lord Milton more than 200 years ago. Walk almost the entire length of the street to return to the Hambro Arms.

JOBS FOR THE GIRLS
West Bay and Bridport

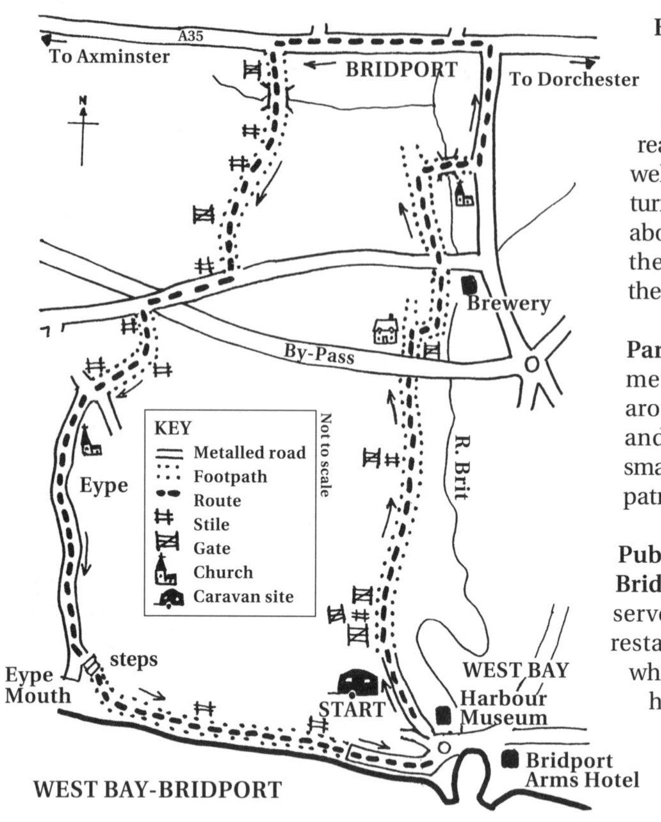

How to get there: West Bay is due south of Bridport and is reached by taking a well-signposted turning at the roundabout on the A35, at the eastern end of the town.

Parking: There is metered parking around the harbour and seafront and a small pub car park for patrons only.

Pub facilities: The Bridport Arms Hotel serves bar food and restaurant meals which include some home-made dishes, a wide selection of fish dishes and several vegetarian options. There is also a children's menu. The bars serve locally-brewed Palmer's beer — our route actually takes you past the brewery, which belongs to a long-established local family firm.

Opening times: Summer 11 am-11 pm Monday-Saturday, 12 noon-10.30 pm Sunday; winter 11 am-2.30 pm, 6.30-11 pm Monday-Friday, 11 am-11 pm Saturday, 12 noon-3 pm, 7-10.30 pm Sunday. Tel: 01308 422994.

Distance: 7 kms (4.4 miles)

Maps: OS Landranger 193 Taunton and Lyme Regis.

Map ref: SY 462 905.

Degree of difficulty: This is an easy and picturesque walk, with varied scenery. It begins at a small fishing port, crosses peaceful water meadows, passes through a market town and returns by way of quiet lanes and Heritage Coast.

The Bridport Arms Hotel, West Bay

Other attractions: The Harbour Museum at West Bay, built as a salt store for the Newfoundland fisheries, now offers displays on the history of Bridport Harbour and the town's longstanding rope and net-making industry. Open 10 am-6 pm daily (summer only). Tel: 01308 420997.

The Bridport Museum in South Street is devoted to the long history of Bridport and is itself housed in a fine Tudor building in the town centre. Tel: 01308 422116.

Details of other attractions are available from **The Tourist Information Centre** opposite the Bridport Museum.

History: West Bay was originally Bridport Harbour and grew up as a tiny port serving the ancient town one and a half miles away and the rope and net manufacturing which have been its staple industry for centuries. The man-made harbour dates from 1740 but the name "West Bay" only from 1884, when the Great Western Railway reached Bridport and officials sought a place-name more in keeping with a holiday resort than a working port.

Bridport is one of the first places to be mentioned in records of Dorset smuggling. Its first Customs officer was appointed as long ago as 1395 and in 1452 a number of Bridport men were among 15 Dorset merchants caught trying to smuggle a shipful of goods out of the country.

When the great smuggling age dawned early in the 18th century, again Bridport was not slow to catch on. In 1719 Customs officers looked on helplessly as a huge cargo of brandy and salt was brought ashore at West Bay and illegally "carried off by great numbers of the country people".

Records of court hearings at Lyme Regis provide confirmation of Bridport's

The harbour at West Bay

interest in smuggling at this period. Of 52 Dorset smugglers named in the minutes of the Lyme Quarter Sessions between 1724 and 1744, three came from Bridport, two from Eype (which also features in the walk) and three from Burton Bradstock, one-and-a-half miles east of West Bay.

When a seizure of goods was made in this area, the usual practice was to bring them before the Lyme Quarter Sessions to be condemned as contraband, after which they would normally be offered for sale by auction. Before this procedure could be followed, however, the officers had to give the owners of the goods a chance to claim it. One West Dorset officer was advised in 1725 that "the people from whom you seize should have all the fair play imaginable". Where the owner's identity was known, he or she would be contacted direct and invited to come and claim their goods; where it was not, notice of the imminent condemnation of the goods in question would be "cried" by the town crier in the nearest market town, such as Bridport or Lyme Regis.

Few if any smugglers turned up to claim their goods, however, for without proof that the duties had been paid, they would merely have compounded their duties. Most preferred a course similar to that followed by Samuel Cossens, of Eype, in 1730 after a seizure of brandy and wine. Told that the consignment was scheduled to be condemned at Lyme Guildhall, Cossens prudently announced that "he thought it best not to come"!

West Bay features in the recollections of the famous Devon and Dorset contraband trader Jack Rattenbury, whose book Memoirs of a Smuggler was published in 1837, when he was still alive. The incident in question occurred in the early 1800s when Rattenbury, whose knowledge of the coast and skills as a ship's pilot were much in demand, "was sent for to Bridport, to take charge of a vessel". That very night, before the vessel left Bridport Harbour, she was boarded by the press gang and Rattenbury found himself (not for the first time) in the hold reluctantly awaiting Naval service.

He managed to bribe his way on to the deck, however, then jumped overboard, only to be recaptured and "carried off in triumph" by the impressment gang. Next morning he persuaded the lieutenant commanding the gang that he could lead him to "some fine young fellows" who would serve the Navy well.

"We then went on shore, and I pointed out a public house to him," says Rattenbury. "But, not finding any there, he began to suspect that my design was to get free, and ordered me down into the boat with the rest of his men. As we were going there I saw my wife coming towards me, and entreated him to let me stop a moment to speak to her; this he gruffly refused, and in an angry tone, again ordered me forward to the boat. As soon as I got on board, I made a start through the water, and up the town. He followed with nine of his men, upon which my wife collared him, and he threw her down; a scuffle then ensued, in which the townspeople took part, while I made my escape, and got clear off."

More than any other place in Dorset, Bridport's contributions to the Dorchester Jail records prove that smuggling was not just men's work. Of the 11 Bridport smugglers listed, no less than five were women. They included shoe thread winders Ruth Hounsell in 1823 and Susan Symes in 1824, twine spinner Joan Stroud (1824) and Charlotte Drake, who was charged with "assaulting and obstructing an Excise officer" in 1817. Another twine spinner, Levia Rutledge, served three months for smuggling in 1820 despite being 60 years old,

The smuggler Jack Rattenbury

widowed and blind!

Of the male Bridport smugglers listed, the luckiest was 26-year-old shoemaker William Powell. His sentence was cut short after five and a half months in 1821 "on account of his Majesty's coronation".

The Walk: The walk begins at the Harbour Museum, a distinctive stone building at the western end of the bridge built to house salt for the Newfoundland cod trade.

Walk straight through the caravan park behind the museum. The River Brit is on the right. Where the road bends to the left, go straight along the paving, then through a thicket. There are water meadows on the right.

Go through the old iron gate (cast locally, as the inscription indicates) and walk straight across the fields, keeping the hedge on your right.

Cross the next stile, which is beside a gate.

After going through the next iron gate,

walk through the meadow, following the sign to Bridport. Climb the stile beside the gate at the far end.

Follow the well-trodden track across the grass and underneath the bypass, which bridges the river just here.

Once under the bridge, head towards the thatched cottage and go through the gate just before it.

Opposite the cottage — called Port Mead — turn right at the signpost towards Bridport.

The pleasant wooded track runs along the River Brit, and you will soon see Palmer's Brewery on the opposite bank, complete with original water wheel.

When you come to a road, go straight across and take the narrow tarmac track beside the river, signposted Bridport.

Bridport Football Club is on the left. The tarmac gives way to gravel and the track passes St Mary's playing fields.

Turn right, over the wooden bridge which is part of the Bridport flood alleviation scheme, and along the tarmac path which leads past the church and on to South Street.

Turn left and head towards the town centre. You will pass the Tourist Information Centre, which is opposite the Bridport Museum, and many interesting small shops.

When you reach the main road (the A35), turn left and walk through the town. Just before the very last house on the left, opposite number 44, turn on to an unmarked path. It has bushes on the left and a wooden fence on the right.

Go through a small iron gate and cross the field, keeping the houses and wall on your left. Cross the narrow wooden bridge over the stream.

In the next field go to the right of the electricity pole, and head towards the stile in the hedge straight ahead of you.

Once over the stile, walk along the wooded path and over the next stile.

Go straight across the next field into the far corner, where there is a five-barred gate in the hedge.

Walk straight across the field (uphill) to the wooden stile which leads on to a lane. Look behind you for a splendid view of Bridport.

Turn right on to the lane and keep going until you have crossed the bridge over the bypass. At the far end of the bridge turn left, over the wooden stile, and continue along the footpath.

At the top of the rise, climb the stile on the right and cross the field towards the church.

Cross the stile on to the lane and, ignoring the private road on the left, follow the sign to Eype and the New Inn.

Pass the church on the left and carry on down the hill. The narrow, twisting lane has an interesting mix of houses and cottages and you will also pass the tiny Eype school, now disused.

Walk on down to the sea at Eype's Mouth, turning left off the lane at some steps just before the beach. Cross the small stream and follow the path up on to the cliff.

You are now on the Dorset Coastal Path which leads back to West Bay. There is a stile about halfway along the path, and one more at the top of the descent to West Bay, where there is also an excellent panoramic view of the harbour and surrounding countryside.

Walk No: 19 — BY THE PIDDLE ON THE FIDDLE

Piddletrentide and Plush

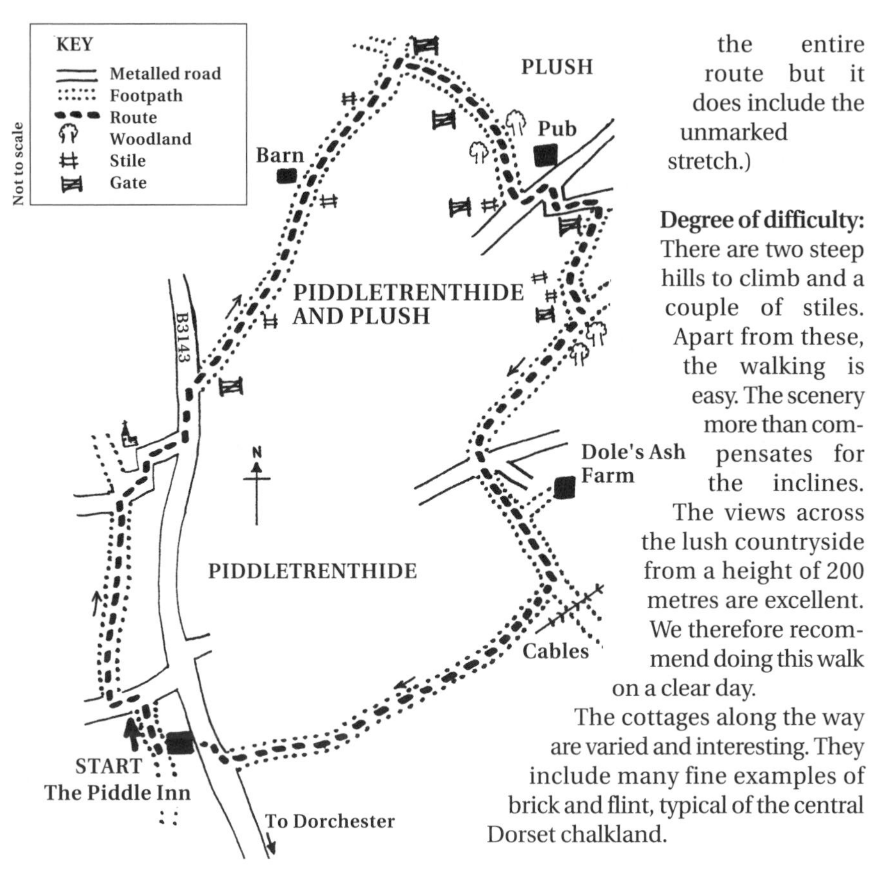

Maps: OS Landranger 194 Dorchester, Weymouth and surrounding area.

Map ref: SY 706 998.

OS Pathfinder 1299 Cerne Abbas.

(NB: Particular care has been taken with the directions for this walk, as the first part is not at all well marked. For this reason we recommend use of the Pathfinder map as well as the Landranger. The Pathfinder does not cover the entire route but it does include the unmarked stretch.)

Degree of difficulty: There are two steep hills to climb and a couple of stiles. Apart from these, the walking is easy. The scenery more than compensates for the inclines. The views across the lush countryside from a height of 200 metres are excellent. We therefore recommend doing this walk on a clear day.

The cottages along the way are varied and interesting. They include many fine examples of brick and flint, typical of the central Dorset chalkland.

How to get there: Piddletrentide lies on the B3143, which can be reached from the A35 to the south via the eastern approach to Dorchester or the B3142 from Puddletown, or to the north from the A352 Sherborne to Dorchester road or the A3030 Sherborne to Sturminster Newton road.

Parking: Walkers may park their cars in the car park of the Piddle Inn providing they are also using the pub.

The Piddle Inn, Piddletrentide

Pub facilities: The Piddle Inn, Piddletrentide, which boasts an apt and distinctive sign featuring night-shirted person with chamber pot, is a friendly village pub, popular with the locals and welcoming to the visitor. It is a free house offering three real ales, a draught cider, two keg beers and two lagers. The small restaurant section offers home-made meals at very reasonable prices and including five or six specials each day. Basket meals, a children's menu and a small selection of wines are also available and there is a children's room. The large and attractive beer garden runs down to the bank of the River Piddle and boasts a slide and Wendy house for the children and a pond with fountain.

Opening times: 11.30 am-2.30 pm and 6.30-11 pm Monday-Friday, 11 am-11 pm Saturday, 12 noon-3 pm and 7-10.30 pm Sunday. Tel: 01300 348468.

The walk also passes **The Brace of Pheasants Inn and Restaurant, Plush.** Tel: 01300 348357.

History: The villagers of the Piddle Valley in central Dorset were early starters in the contraband trade, which was already big business in these parts by about 1720, a time usually regarded as the dawn of the great smuggling age. As early as 1718, it was reported that the village of Piddle, or Puddletown, was "on the smugglers' high road". The following year there were two major incidents at Collier's Piddle (now Piddletrentide).

The first of these occurred in November 1719, when sizeable quantities of smuggled goods were seized from Mr Harry Constantine, the village squire, and William Dolling, of the Rose and Crown.The contraband included bohea tea, coffee, cocoa beans, brandy, white pepper, muslin, canvas and French handkerchiefs, together worth the then

Piddletrentide, scene of smuggling incidents in 1719

very considerable sum of £310. Harry Constantine protested that the goods had been lodged on his premises without permission but officials reported that "it is the opinion of most gentlemen in the country that he must know of it". Orders went out from the Customs department for Constantine and his coachman, John Harding, to be prosecuted.

Within a month, Customs officials were back at Piddletrentide searching for parcels of newly-landed goods, several of which were supposed to have been hidden in houses there. This time, however, the locals received advance warning of the raid and staged a mass evacuation. When the Customs men arrived, they found the entire village deserted and every house locked up. Even the parish constable and the tithingman were nowhere to be found. This was a clever move on the part of the villagers, because without these parish officials, the Customs men had no authority to enter or search any property. They waited several hours until darkness fell but still no-one appeared. Eventually they were forced, in the words of the Weymouth Collector of Customs, Philip Taylor, to "return without doing anything, this being a case that frequently happens, and the smugglers take all advantage of the least misconduct of the officers".

Taylor's own superiors, the Commissioners of Customs in London, were not completely satisfied by this explanation and requested a further report from their man in Weymouth. This time Taylor wrote: "It would have been inappropriate for all the officers of this town to guard the houses all night by reason of the danger of the mob, who appeared in great numbers and are always ready to insult us when they can do it undiscovered. It was most certainly the contrivance of the smugglers to send the parish officers from home, but they (and

Church and cottages at Piddletrentide

indeed the greatest part of the country) are all so firmly linked together in the smuggling trade that it will be impossible to prove the collusion on them."

Over the hill at Cerne Abbas things were much the same. Here a merchant family, the Randells, were heavily involved in smuggling. There were two seizures of linen cloth from Thomas Randell's home in 1718, while a defiant George Randell warned Customs officers that they had "no authority to stop or examine any person or goods on the road and that if we do not desist from so doing it will be attended with the murder of some or other of us".

A description of the local smugglers at work during this period was given by Edmund Coish, who lived at a place "through which the smugglers' troops do frequently pass". Coish was a man of "indifferent reputation and circumstance" but also of loose tongue, as Philip Taylor discovered. He deliberately plied Coish with October, the strongest beer available, named after the month in which it was brewed, and encouraged him to talk.

"I liquored him with October and plied him with the usual questions I make to the country people of the price of wine and brandy and how they are supplied with the same," he wrote. "Whereto he replied that there was great running in their country and that the Tuesday before, soon after day, he saw between 20 and 30 men armed with clubs and staves and other weapons come from towards Cerne, where he was told they had conducted some goods for Mr George Randell, but in what house the same was lodged and whither it was removed thence, as usual he could not tell."

Such was life in Piddletrentide as the great smuggling age got underway. It was a way of life which continued in this area for more than 100 years.

The Walk: Take the bridle path at the rear of the pub. It runs parallel to the village street. Cross the bridge and follow the track.

When you come to a road, turn left, then after about 50 yards, turn right, following the blue arrow. Walk straight along the track, which is grass in places, until you reach a metalled road. There is a Kiddles Farm sign on the left and the church is visible straight ahead.

Turn right on to the road and walk to

the main street, then left as far as the wooden footpath sign which you will see on your right just before the road sign.

The path goes up the side of the hill at an angle. Go through the gate and follow the chalk track. As you climb, a pretty view of the village will unfold behind you.

At the top, climb the stile in the wire fence — there is no footpath sign.

The path goes diagonally to the right across the field to an old tin trough and pile of flints — the only landmarks at the time of writing.

The footpath then leads across the field to the top corner nearest the barn, but walkers are asked to use their discretion and if necessary walk around the edge rather than trample the crop.

Head towards the barn and you will find a stile with a yellow arrow in the corner of the field.

Climb the stile and follow the edge of the field, keeping the hedge on your right.

Just after the overhead cables, at the crest of the hill, the hedge bears to the left. Offset from the corner is a wooden stile marked with a yellow arrow.

Climb the stile and you will find yourself in the top corner of a field. There will be some fine views over the surrounding countryside.

Walk down the slope.

The path leaves this field on the right hand edge through a five-bar gate.

Go through the gate and follow the track down the slope.

Continue through the next gate where there are far reaching views, and on downhill to the bottom of the track. Climb the unusual iron stile next to the gate, and turn left along the road. You will soon reach the Brace of Pheasants Inn and Restaurant.

Follow the road round to the right, through the village and past the Plush roadsign. Go past a house called Miller's Barn on the left, and a short way beyond you will see a gate on the right with a yellow arrow on it.

Once through the gate, follow the track up the side of the hill. You will now have a good view over the pub and village.

Climb the stile and continue up the hill. Cross the next stile, which bears a yellow arrow, and walk straight on until you see an iron gate.

Go through the gate and walk towards the trees, in which is Thorncombe Barn. Just before you reach the trees, turn right on to the bridleway which crosses our path. There are no signs at all, but there should be a track to follow.

Keep the hedge on your left as you walk down the incline. The views are excellent. Where the hedge ends, carry straight on along the bridleway, which is marked with a blue arrow.

On reaching a road, go straight across on to the signposted bridleway to the right of the Dole's Ash Farm track.

Keeping the hedge to your right, walk on. When you reach a track to the house, ignore it and go straight on.

Fifty yards before some overhead cables, turn right along an unmarked track between hedges. This is a pleasant, easy-to-walk path which leads straight downhill to the main road.

At the end of the track, turn right on to the village street and walk back to the Piddle Inn.

Walk No: 20

LIGHTS ACROSS THE VALLEY
Spyway and Eggardon Hill

Distance: 5 kms (3.1 miles)

Maps: OS Landranger 194 Dorchester, Weymouth and surrounding area. Map ref: SY 528 934.

Degree of difficulty: The climb to the top of Eggardon is fairly steep but the route has been carefully planned to place the steepest gradient on a downhill section! The route passes through farmland and has superb views in all directions.

There is a short section along a minor road but visibility is good and traffic limited.

We recommend, however, that dogs are not taken on this walk, even on a lead, as there are so many sheep.

How to get there: Spyway is a hamlet in the parish of Askerswell, situated a few miles north-east of Bridport and north of the A35 trunk road between Bridport and Dorchester. From the A35, it can be reached via Askerswell village, which is well-signposted. For those approaching from the Dorchester direction, the old Roman road near Winterbourne Abbas offers a quieter alternative, following the ridge to Eggardon, where a left turn leads downhill to Spyway.

Parking: Walkers intending to use the Spyway Inn are also welcome to use one of the pub's two car parks providing they check first with licensees Don and Jackie Roderick or their staff. This check is specifically requested by the licensees because car park space is limited and sometimes needed for delivery lorries or coaches; cars which have been parked and left can cause problems. Elsewhere in the village, there is virtually nowhere to park due to the narrow-

The Spyway Inn, near Askerswell

ness of the lanes. If the pub car park is full — or you do not plan to use the inn — we suggest parking in the Eggardon lay-by (map reference 546 944). It is on the route and the walk could be started from there.

Pub facilities: The Spyway Inn is an attractive old building dating back several hundred years and licensed since 1745 at least. Until 1905 the pub was attached to the village smithy, hence its earlier name, The Three Horsehoes, which it retained until 1974. It also has a strong smuggling tradition, reflected until recently by an the interesting pub sign featuring cutlass-wielding smugglers. The sign has now been replaced by one featuring the pub itself.

The Spyway is a free house with a large beer garden, three bars and a collection of 210 tea cups hanging from the ceiling of the Horseshoes bar. The tempting menu includes home-made food and a variety of ploughman's lunches. Beer includes three cask-conditioned ales. And so to the wine…the 45 wines on offer, including 21 country wines, made this pub the very first winner of the Carlsberg-Tetley national pub wine list of the year title in 1995. It is also one of very few Dorset pubs with a star rating in the Good Pub Guide. Opening times: 10.30 am-2.30 pm and 6-11 pm Monday-Saturday, 12 noon-3 pm and 7-10.30 pm Sunday. Tel: 01308 485250.

History: What tales of smugglers and smuggling could be told by the walls of the Spyway Inn, if only they could talk! This ancient pub — formerly the Three Horseshoes — stands on an old smuggling route which ran northwards from the beaches of Swyre and Burton Bradstock. Generations of contraband carriers passed this way, conveying their cargoes of spirits, wine, tea and tobacco to Yeovil, Bath, Bristol and perhaps even London or Worcester and the Midlands.

Years ago, apparently, there was

The former inn sign at Spyway featuring smugglers at work

another pub, the Blue Boar, across the valley from the Three Horseshoes, near the present A35 trunk road. According to local tradition, the two inns served as signalling posts for smuggling gangs. "You can see us quite clearly from the hilltop on the main road," said Spyway Inn landlord Don Roderick. "The story is that the smugglers used to make sure the way was clear by signalling to each other with lanterns across the valley." The Blue Boar has long since been demolished.

Eggardon Hill — also a major feature of this walk — makes its own contributions to smuggling history. Older customers have told Mr Roderick that there used to be caves on the hill which once provided handy hiding places for newly-landed contraband. The goods would be stored there until opportunity presented itself for the smugglers to begin the next stage of the operation. "The caves were eventually filled in for safety reasons," said Mr Roderick.

Eggardon also attracted the interest of Isaac Gulliver, a man described by contemporary Customs officers as "one of the greatest and most notorious smugglers in the West of England, and particularly in the spirits and tea trades". Gulliver's main operational bases were 30 miles away in the Kinson-Wimborne area but his contraband empire stretched well beyond Dorset in every direction and he owned property in four counties. At some time in the 1780s, he added Eggardon to his scattered landholdings. He purchased the farm known as North Eggardon from his friend the Rev William Chafin, himself at that time the owner of Chettle House, near Blandford, which has a secret underground passage and is today owned by descendants of Isaac Gulliver (see Farnham-Chettle walk)!

On the summit of Eggardon, Gulliver's men planted a clump of trees and constructed an octagonal bank and ditch to shelter them from the wild winds sweeping in from the sea. The purpose of this plantation, five miles inland and 820 feet above sea level, was to provide a landmark for the crews of Gulliver's smuggling vessels as they approached the coast. For a time the smuggler's saplings grew and prospered. But legend has it that word of their purpose eventually reached official ears and the trees were felled on Government orders. Traces of the octagonal bank and ditch can still be seen, however.

Eggardon's other defences — the great green ramparts which once supported the wooden walls of an Iron Age village

Eggardon Hill

— predate Isaac Gulliver's efforts by 2,000 years. The hillfort was occupied from about 300 BC but the defences failed to keep out the invading Romans, who captured the site in the first century AD. Geologically, Eggardon is the last frontier of the chalk landmass which covers much of southern and south-eastern England.

The Walk: Turn right out of the pub car park and walk as far as the road junction. Turn left through the wooden gate. There is a bridleway sign, and another marked "South Eggardon Farm".

The metalled path has fields of sheep on the left, and Eggardon is straight ahead.

After passing a thatched cottage on the right, look out for a blue arrow and signpost on the left, pointing to North Eggardon. Follow the sign through a gate, and downhill across the field, going through the gate on the far side.

The path skirts the lake and bears right. Keep the wire fence on your right.

Go through the wooden gate, turn left, and go to the five-bar gate in the hedge ahead of you.

Follow the path, which has a stream on its left, and go through the next gate, which is a small, wooden one. Head across the grass towards the buildings.

Go through the gate, pass the cottage on the right and follow the track and the blue arrows through the farmyard.

Once past the buildings, go through the gate opposite the wooden signpost, in the direction of Eggardon.

The track, with a hedge on its left, climbs towards the top of Eggardon. Go through the gate near the summit.

Turn to the right and either walk along this more sheltered lower path, or alternatively climb to the very top. Either way you will have glorious views over surrounding countryside to Bridport and the coast.

On reaching a gate, stile and National Trust sign, climb the stile and turn

Entrance to Eggardon Hill

right.

Follow the grassy track along the crest of the hill. The view is superb.

Cross the next stile and turn right along the road. There is not much traffic, and the road leads downhill.

Watch out for a red gas pipeline sign in a passing place on the right hand side of the road, and shortly afterwards go through the metal gate on the same side. It has a blue arrow on the *inside.*

Go through the gate and walk diagonally to the left, as indicated by the bridleway sign. The track is cut into the hillside, and passes between the wooden electricity poles.

Follow the blue arrows, keeping the wire fence on the right.

The track goes down the slope towards the farm.

Go through the gate, turn right, then left, skirting the farm, and you will soon be back on the farm track on which you walked earlier. Go through the gate and turn left on to it and return to Spyway.

Walk No: 21 A JOB FOR THE BOW STREET RUNNERS Wool and Coombe Keynes

Distance: 8 kms (5 miles)

Maps: OS Landranger 194 Dorchester, Weymouth and surrounding area. Map ref: SY 842 867.

Degree of difficulty: This is a very easy, pleasant walk through the village and across undulating countryside. The back streets of Wool are attractive, with thatched cottages and ducks in the stream and gardens.

There is only one stile, and no steep hills.

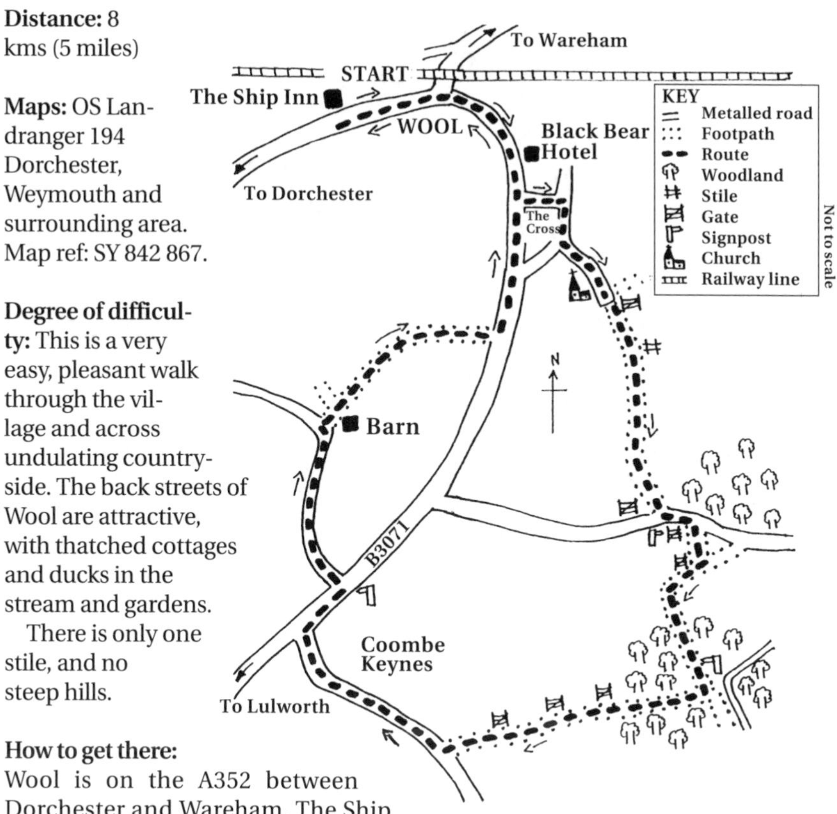

How to get there:
Wool is on the A352 between Dorchester and Wareham. The Ship Inn is on the western side of the level crossing.

Parking: The Ship Inn has two large car parks and walkers are welcome to use them providing they also intend to use the pub. There is also a small public car park in The Cross — on our route at map reference 847 867— and ample street parking.

Pub facilities: The Ship Inn, a Badger Inn, is not the old fashioned roadside inn of its smuggling landlord Tom Lucas's time (or even of a few years ago) but a large and homely pub-restaurant with a broad and inviting menu catering for most tastes and all appetites. Meals are served all day, portions are generous and prices reasonable. Beers served include two real ales.

The large beer garden is ideal for train-spotting as well as summer drinking and there are swings, a slide and a trampoline for children. The pub has

The Ship Inn, Wool

ample car parking.

Opening times: 11 am-11 pm Monday-Saturday, 12 noon-10.30 pm Sunday. Tel: 01929 462247.

History: Wool's proximity to Lulworth and the coast guaranteed it a prominent role in the smuggling business. For many years it was on one of the regular routes inland and cargoes frequently passed this way. Most got through successfully and without incident but there were exceptions, as in Woolbridge Lane, north of the village, in 1779, when a "large and desperate" gang of smugglers clashed with revenue officials and soldiers from Dorchester. In the course of the battle at least one smuggler was shot dead and, in the words of a contemporary newspaper, "many more were dangerously wounded". The seizure included 300 gallons of brandy and gin, 2,300 pounds of tea and 32 smugglers' horses.

Coombe Keynes, which also features in this walk, was the location of another incident in 1767, when Customs officers discovered a large quantity of tea in Coombe Wood, west of the village. The goods had been landed near Swanage some time earlier from a Devon smuggling vessel which had run into contrary winds in the Channel. The tea was stored in quarries until a gang arrived from Devon to collect it and it was on the return journey that they took cover in Coombe Wood until it was safe to continue. After the officers discovered the tea, one went off to fetch a wagon, while another, Thomas Croombs, moved 12 bags to another spot to hinder any rescue attempt.

The rescue soon came. No sooner had Croombs moved the bags than "a gang of 28 men, all on horseback, dressed in carters' frocks, and unknown, came to the officers and threatened to kill them if they offered to touch a bag of the tea; which they immediately began to load on their horses; but in such confusion that they never missed the 12 bags carried off as above; and on their going away in triumph, gave (as they called it) the three officers two bags each". The noise attracted the gamekeeper from the Weld estate at Lulworth but his arrival made no difference. The smugglers simply confiscated his gun and "throwed all the gunpowder he had about him away".

The Ship Inn at Wool was a popular smugglers' pub and in the 1820s the landlord himself, Tom Lucas, was one of the leaders of a notorious local gang. These men had a particular reputation for violence and possessed a formidable armoury which included pistols, swords, bludgeons, poles and the relatively new swingle, a nasty flail-type weapon which could be flung whiplash-style around someone's body, with deadly effect. For some time this gang ran riot on the Isle of Purbeck, causing serious injury to several officers of the recently-formed Coastguard. Eventually, after a clash which caused two deaths and many other casualties near St Alban's Head in 1827, several of the gang leaders were identified and the Bow Street Runners summoned from London to deal with them.

They arrived at the Ship well-armed and with their tactics well thought out. It was 2 am when they knocked on the door.

"Who's there?" barked Lucas, gruffly.

"It's only me, Mr Lucas," said one of the Runners in a high-pitched voice. "Mrs Smith's little girl. I want a little drop of brandy for mother for she is bad in her bowels."

Lucas opened the door and was instantly arrested and carried off to Dorchester Jail, where he soon found himself reunited with five of his comrades. The charges against four of the six were later dropped; Lucas and one other were tried but acquitted. In the prison registers, Lucas is described as a shoemaker, aged 45, with sandy hair, red whiskers, a short greying beard, scarred face and a mole on his right cheek.

Lucas is not the only Wool smuggler listed in the prison registers. Others are Edith Mead, aged 63, and William Hurst, 39, who served six and seven months respectively for smuggling in 1803; 37-year-old labourer George Langdon, caught conveying smuggled brandy in 1813; and Thomas Stickland, 25, also a labourer, sentenced to two months hard labour in 1825 for making a light on the coast as a signal to smugglers. From Coombe Keynes in 1832 came thatcher Charles Bascombe, 26, charged with assisting in the landing of contraband, being armed with offensive weapons and assaulting Customs officers; and from neighbouring Winfrith, carpenter George Talbot, aged 19, who served nine months after failing to pay a £100 smuggling fine in 1833.

The Walk: Turn left out of the Ship Inn car park and walk along the pavement. At the junction do not cross the railway line, but go straight on along Station Road.

After passing a pub called the Black Bear, take the next turning on the left, called The Cross. At the end of The Cross turn right and walk along the lane, which is bordered on the left by a stream. The cottage gardens boast ducks as well as roses!

Take the first turning on the left, which is on a bend. It is a cul-de-sac called Church Lane.

There are many attractive cottages to look at. Pass the church and walk right to the end of the lane.

Enter the field on the right and walk in the direction shown by the arrow on the electricity pole.

Follow the track across the field towards the clump of trees. There are views behind to the River Frome.

On reaching the hedge, cross the wooden stile, and follow the yellow arrow across the next field. The track leads up a rise.

On reaching the next hedge, go through the gap, and follow the track straight ahead along the edge of the next field.

Keep the hedge on your left, and on reaching a gap in it, go through and follow the path across the field.

The Purbeck Hills are ahead, and there are also pleasant views over the rolling countryside to the right.

At the gate, turn left on to the lane.

After walking a short distance, look out for a gate on the right and a wooden signpost marked "Bridleway".

Following the blue arrow, go straight across the field to the gate. Go through, and turn right on to the track.

The sunken path passes between hedgerows. Follow it uphill and into coniferous woodland.

Continue through the trees until you reach a signpost at the bottom of a slope.

Turn right, along the track signposted Coombe Keynes.

The wide track passes through mixed woodland.

The wood ends at the top of a rise. Go through the gate marked with a blue arrow, and cross the field, keeping close to the fence on the right.

Follow the blue waymarker and go through the next gate and across another field following the track.

At the bottom of the slope, go through the gate, and along a gravel track.

Walk to the end of the track and then turn right, on to the metalled road.

The lane passes through Coombe Keynes. Walk right to the end, and at the junction turn right, on to the B3071. A little to the west of here is Coombe Wood, scene of a smuggling incident in 1767 (see History section).

Alongside the B3071 is a very wide grassy verge for safe walking. After a short distance you will reach a signpost. Cross the road, and take the side road to New Buildings.

The lane leads downhill and gives good views ahead.

Where the road bears left, leave it, and go straight on along the gravel track. Ignore the gate and footpath sign on the left.

There is a barn called New Buildings on the right.

The track leads uphill and curves around the rejoin the B3071 just outside Wool.

Turn left and follow the road back to the car.

MOONFLEET
Langton Herring and The Fleet

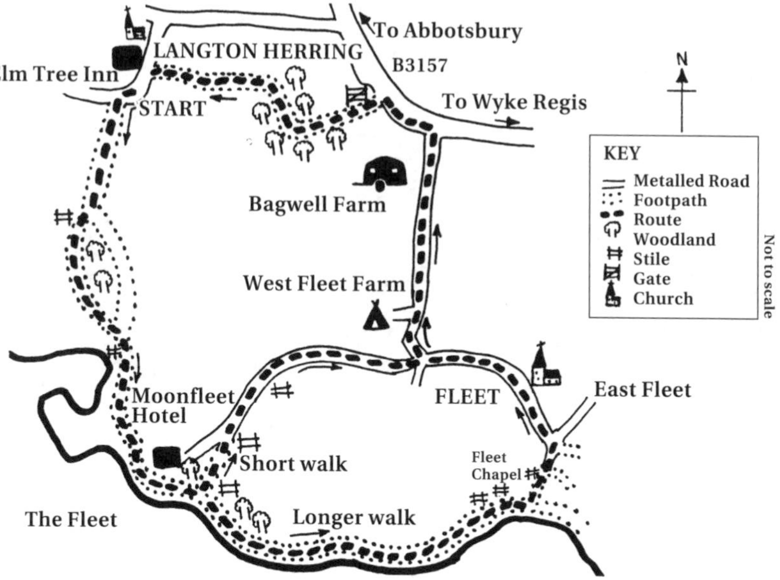

LANGTON HERRING-THE FLEET

To Abbotsbury
LANGTON HERRING
B3157
Elm Tree Inn
START
To Wyke Regis
N
KEY
Metalled Road
Footpath
Route
Woodland
Stile
Gate
Church
Not to scale
Bagwell Farm
West Fleet Farm
Moonfleet Hotel
FLEET
East Fleet
Short walk
Fleet Chapel
The Fleet
Longer walk

Distance: Longer walk approx 8 kms (5 miles); shorter walk approx 5 kms (3.1 miles).

Maps: OS Landranger 194 Dorchester, Weymouth and surrounding area. Map ref: SY 615 824.

Degree of difficulty: Apart from a few stiles, this walk is an easy one, with varied scenery ranging from woodland to close views of the Fleet. On clear days it is possible to see Portland in one direction and beyond Golden Cap to the south Devon coast in the other.

There are a couple of muddy patches during wet spells.

How to get there: From the A35 Dorchester to Bridport road, turn south at Winterbourne Abbas towards Portesham and Abbotsbury. At Portesham, turn left on to the B3157. Take the second signposted turning to Langton Herring on the right. The walk begins at the Elm Tree Inn near the centre of the village.

Parking: Walkers can use the paddock extension of the car park of the Elm Tree Inn providing they also patronise the pub. There are few alternatives to this as the village streets are narrow with very few parking places.

Pub facilities: The Elm Tree Inn — a

The Elm Tree Inn, Langton Herring

Greenalls pub signposted from the B3157 — is a very old and attractive building with a well-tended garden complete with picnic tables. Inside, timber beams are much in evidence, providing a delightful olde world atmosphere. At least one beam is an old ship's mast with two hooks on it. Legend has it that a fisherman was hanged from these hooks for lying about his catch!

Other features include a well under the kitchen and a large open fireplace with original bread oven and, reputedly, a tunnel leading from here to the church next door. This may have been a smugglers' tunnel or escape route. Smugglers would certainly have used this pub as a meeting place a couple of centuries ago, as did Portland spy ring members Ethel Gee and Harry Houghton before their arrest in 1961 for selling naval secrets to Russia.

The Elm Tree has a wide range of quality meals and snacks and a wine list. Drinks include two real ales, two lagers and cider, plus a wide range of soft drinks to cater for the driver. Children are allowed in the front bar.

Opening Times: 10.30 am-3 pm and 6-11 pm Monday-Saturday, 12 noon-10.30 pm Sunday. Tel: 01305 871257.

The Moonfleet Manor Hotel, formerly Fleet House, is a mainly 18th century building which takes its present name from John Meade Falkner's famous novel Moonfleet. The hotel is open all year round. Facilities include indoor and outdoor children's play areas and swimming pool area.

Opening times: Restaurant 7-9 pm; hotel bar from 6 pm; bar in the adjoining Ball Park 10.30 am-11 pm. Tel: 01305 786948.

Optional extras: Binoculars for keen birdwatchers, as there are many rare species.

History: Some years ago the occupants of an old cottage near the Square at Langton Herring set about raising the flagstones which formed their floor in order to carry out repair work. To their surprise, they discovered that the removal of certain stones opened up a forgotten tunnel which led under the floor and away towards another part of the village. The same cottage had a large chimney inside which, hidden from view but within reach for an adult arm, was a ledge wide enough to accommodate a row of bottles. The couple assumed that both the tunnel and the chimney ledge were evidence that their home was once occupied by smugglers — and they were probably right, as tunnels and hiding places such as secret rooms and cupboards are a common feature of older properties in towns and villages known to have been smuggling communities.

The records of Dorchester Prison leave no doubt about the strength of Langton Herring's smuggling connections. Between 1815 and 1834, the village provided no less than 12 inmates for the County Gaol on smuggling-related charges. Two others came from Fleet. Five of the Langton Herring smugglers were members of the Vivian family, including 14-year-old Martha Vivian, who went to prison for smuggling in 1826, and fisherman John Vivian, aged 17, who in 1818 was sentenced to three months hard labour for "making a light and fire as a signal to person or persons on board a smuggling vessel".

Another name associated with smuggling at Langton Herring is Whittle and two members of this family are also listed in the prison records. One of them, William Whittle, a 23-year-old seaman, was sentenced to death at the Dorset Assizes in 1834 for "smuggling, assaulting preventive officers and feloniously assembling to the number of three or more to assist in landing and running prohibited goods". Fortunately for Whittle, he was later reprieved and his sentence reduced to one of transportation to the colonies (probably Australia) for ten years.

A worse fate awaited 31-year-old Langton Herring labourer Thomas Traverse, who was imprisoned for smuggling in 1817. The prison records tell us that he was "short breathed from an asthma and departed this life — his body was delivered to his friends".

Reports from Weymouth Custom House provide further evidence. In 1717 three officers investigating a landing of contraband on the Chesil Beach near Fleet in the early hours were set upon by "30 men in disguise, armed with clubs and other weapons, who drove them from the place". In 1746 the Langton Herring riding officer Edward Bayley was "obstructed while attempting to do his duty" and in the same year smugglers broke into the home of his colleague John Moies and retrieved 134 pounds of smuggled tea which had been seized from them earlier.

A major feature of this walk is the Fleet, whose passive waters, sheltered from the English Channel by the Chesil Beach, proved a great asset to local smugglers. If danger threatened they could sink their tubs of spirits in the Fleet knowing that they were unlikely to be swept away on a rough sea. It is said that smugglers and fisherman landing on the Chesil Beach on a moonless night could tell roughly where they were by the size of the pebbles, which get progressively bigger towards the eastern end.

Boats beached beside the Fleet

Within a short distance of the Fleet is the Moonfleet Manor Hotel, formerly Fleet House, a mainly 18th century building which takes its present name from John Meade Falkner's famous novel Moonfleet. A mile to the east are the remains of the original Fleet church, which also features in the novel. It is here that the young John Trenchard sits on a tomb above the Mohun family vault, where the local smugglers hid their tubs of spirits. When the church is flooded, the kegs are heard bumping against each other in the vault.

The old Fleet church serves only as a mortuary chapel now, having been wrecked in 1824 by a great storm which swept away much of the village. The present church, Holy Trinity, was built a few years later.

The Walk: Turn right out of the pub car park and walk along the road, past the cul-de-sac sign. The road bears right at Lerret Cottage.

Just past the Methodist Church turn left at the wooden signpost.

The unmade track has a dry stone wall on the right and if you look back you will have excellent fine weather views to Golden Cap and the Devon coast.

As you walk over the rise you will have your first sighting of the Fleet and Chesil Bank.

There is a choice at this point. You can either climb the stile on the right and walk along the edge of the wood, or carry on along the gravel track. The paths rejoin at the bottom of the hill.

Climb the stile and join the Dorset coast path. Follow the sign marked East Fleet. There is a stone wall to the left and at harvest-time there are lots of interesting machines to watch.

The lagoon – home to a rich variety of birdlife – is very close on the right.

As you cross Herbury, Gore Cove comes into view. Once over the stile, walk along the beach. These lower reaches of the Fleet are tidal, so the amount of space will vary!

At the far end of the beach look for the track leading to the top of the low cliff. It is marked by a wooden post with a yellow arrow.

Once at the top, you will soon see the Moonfleet Manor Hotel on the left complete with yacht weather vane. It is open to walkers, serving morning coffee, lunch, snacks, etc.

Opposite the hotel is a sign drawing attention to the Fleet Sanctuary Nature Reserve — the second oldest reserve in Britain. These days The Fleet's shallow waters are recognised as a wetland of international importance.

Climb the stile and cross the field where there is another stile and a footbridge over a stream.

At the signpost in memory of "Simon — who despite his handicap was dedicated to the Heritage Coast" — climb the stile and, for the **shorter route**, head in the direction of Fleet Road.

Once over the next stile, follow the signpost pointing to Fleet Lane (sic — one sign says "Road", the other says "Lane"). After the next stile you will be on the hotel road. Turn right and walk up the hill to the junction. Just before you reach it look out for the Victorian postbox and intricate metal fence.

Turn left and pass the West Fleet campsite. The footpath follows the edge of the campsite but does not enter it.

The track leads uphill to the main road.

Turn left on to the B3157, and pass the Bagwell Farm Touring Park.

After walking along the verge for a short distance, go through the wooden gate in the layby on the left. It is marked with a blue arrow and the bridleway passes through mixed woodland. It may be muddy in places.

Where the track branches, bear right, following the blue arrow. The path leads uphill and, where the trees end, bears left, becoming a grassy path between fences.

The path leads through a farmyard and then out on to the road, almost opposite the Elm Tree Inn.

For the **longer route**, from Simon's signpost continue along the coast path in the direction of Weymouth.

After about a mile the path turns inland into a thicket and over a plank and stile. Cross this stile and the next one and follow the sign to East Fleet and Church.

Cross the grass and walk in the direction of Fleet and Chickerell. Follow the path, which skirts the remains of the old Fleet church, wrecked in the great storm of 1824 and subsequently made famous through J Meade Falkner's novel Moonfleet.

Turn on to the lane, via the gate and stile, and walk to the junction.

Turn left on to the road, which leads uphill and passes the 19th century church on the right.

Rejoin the shorter route by turning right at the top of the hill and passing the West Fleet campsite.

Walk No: 23 'ON THE SMUGGLERS' HIGH ROAD'
Puddletown Forest and Higher Bockhampton

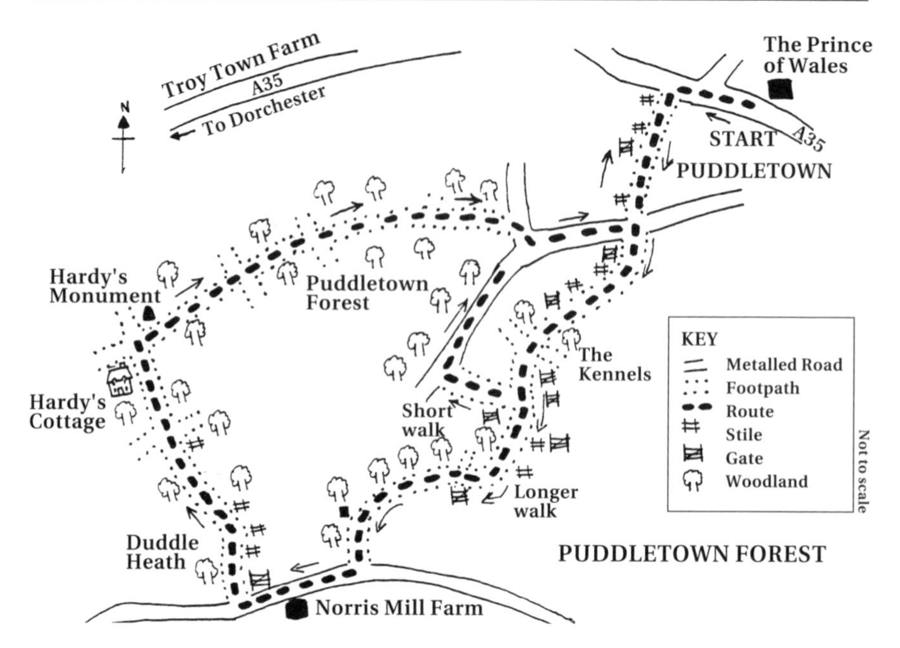

Distance: Longer walk approx 9 kms (5.6 miles); shorter walk approx 3 kms (2 miles).

Maps: OS Landranger 194 Dorchester, Weymouth and surrounding area.
Map Ref: SY 756 946.

Degree of difficulty: This is a very pleasant walk through the contrasting scenery of fields and woodland. The hills are gentle and the shade of the forest makes it a good choice for a hot day.

How to get there: Puddletown is on the A35 road five miles east of Dorchester.

Parking: Walkers intending to use the Prince of Wales Inn – situated beside the A35 – may use the customers' car park. There is also limited parking in some of the village sidestreets or in a lay-by a few hundred yards on the Dorchester side of the traffic lights.

Pub facilities: The Prince of Wales Inn at Puddletown, a Hall and Woodhouse pub, serves real ale and a wide range of food at all times. Facilities include a car park with 50 spaces and a beer garden with children's play area. Children can also use the lounge bar if eating. Dogs are allowed in the public bar only. The present pub dates from 1930, when the previous building was burnt down. Landlady Christina Shawyer says there has been a pub on the site for 400 years. Opening times: 11 am-3 pm and 6.30-11 pm Monday-Saturday,

The Prince of Wales, Puddletown

12 noon-3 pm and 7-10.30 pm Sunday. Tel: 01305 848222.

Other attractions: Ilsington House, close to the centre of Puddletown, was built in 1690 by the seventh Earl of Huntingdon. It has strong royal connections, having been leased by royal command to the king's senior equerry Major General Thomas Garth from 1780 to 1830. Several members of the royal family stayed there during this period. Ilsington was also the childhood home of the equerry's adopted son Tommy Garth, illegitimate son of Princess Sophia, one of George III's daughters. Edward VII and Thomas and Florence Hardy stayed there a century later. The house was opened to the public for the first time in 1991 by owners Peter and Penelope Duff, who have a remarkable collection of modern art. Open 2-6 pm Sunday, Wednesday, Thursday and bank holiday Mondays, May-September. Tel: 01305-848454.

Hardy's Cottage, Higher Bockhampton, the birthplace of Thomas Hardy. The thatched cob cottage – now a National Trust property – was built by the writer's great-grandfather and occupied by the family from 1801. Two of Hardy's early novels, Under the Greenwood Tree and Far from the Madding Crowd, were written here. Open April-October 11-6 pm (or dusk if earlier) daily except Thursday. Tel: 01305 262366.

History: Puddletown is the Weatherbury of Thomas Hardy's Far From the Madding Crowd and the area's smuggling connections were not lost on the great Dorset writer. In his personal notebooks he reveals that his own grandfather (who came from Puddletown) used to hide tubs of spirits in a dark closet at his cottage at Higher Bockhampton. The closet was big enough for 80 tubs, each containing about four and a quarter gallons of extremely strong brandy.

"The spirits often smelt all over the house, being proof, and had to be lowered for drinking," wrote Hardy. "The tubs,or little elongated barrels, were of thin staves with wooden hoops. (I remember one of them which had been turned into a bucket by knocking out one head and putting a handle.) They were brought at night by men on horseback, 'slung', or in carts. A whiplash across the window pane would wake my grandfather at two or three in the morning, and he would dress and go down. Not a soul was there, but a heap of tubs loomed up in front of the door. He would set to work and stow them away in the dark closet aforesaid, and nothing more would happen till dusk the following evening, when groups of dark, long-bearded fellows would arrive, and carry off the tubs in twos and fours slung over their shoulders."

By letting him sleep until the moment of their departure, the smugglers ensured that Hardy senior would be unable to identify them in the unfortunate event of anyone being caught.

Hardy's grandfather moved to Higher Bockhampton in 1801 but there is ample evidence of smuggling in the area at least 80 years before that. As early as 1717, at the very dawn of the "great smuggling age", the Collector of Customs at Weymouth, Philip Taylor, was appealing to the Board of Customs in London for permission to employ additional riding officers at Dorchester, Cerne Abbas and "Piddle" or "Piddle Town", as Puddletown was then known. "The smugglers ride with companies of armed men, 20, 30 or 40 in a gang, and very dangerous to the officers in the night time," Taylor warned. But only one additional appointment was allowed.

The following year, Taylor reported that Puddletown was on a major smuggling route – "on the smugglers' high road", as he put it. He named innkeeper John Tuckett of Puddletown as a "notorious smuggler" and his pub, the King's Arms, as "a common receptacle for runned goods". In fact, Tuckett was caught red-handed with contraband brandy in 1718. In an effort to defend himself, he promptly bought some more from Weymouth's Customs warehouse (it had probably been seized from some other smuggler) and insisted this was his usual practice.

In 1719 Taylor named a man called Roper as a "noted smuggler at Piddle". But when officers searched his hay wagon they found only hay on board. Roper the smuggler may have been the Richard Roper mentioned in a census of Puddletown compiled by the local vicar in 1724. He lived in a house at The Green with his wife Ann, their two small children and his mother-in-law. The same census shows John Tuckett at the King's Arms with his wife Joan, three children and four servants.

Other Puddletown smugglers included George House, of Norris Mill, who was sentenced to 18 months in Dorchester Jail in 1791 for assaulting and obstructing an Excise officer, and John Knight, of Troy Town, charged with conveying smuggled brandy in 1813 but released without prosecution after three months in custody.

The Walk: Outside the pub, cross the road and walk towards the traffic lights. On the left, opposite the turning to Blandford, is the site of the King's Arms, demolished a few years ago following a fire. This was the pub kept in 1718 by the

Thomas Hardy's birthplace at Higher Bockhampton

smuggler John Tuckett, who turned it into "a common receptacle for runned goods".

Carry straight on in the direction of Dorchester and after a few yards take the footpath on the left, immediately after some houses, signposted to White Hill. Climb the wooden stile and follow the path along the edge of the field, ignoring the stile on your left.

At the top of the rise go over the wooden stile and continue straight on, beside the school fence. Pass through the metal gate and straight up the rise along the edge of the field.

Cross another wooden stile, which is within a few yards of a metalled road. Across the road, directly opposite, you will see double metal gates. Go through the gates and climb the wooden stile which lies slightly ahead and to the right. It is marked with a blue bridleway arrow. The path now crosses two fields (with a stile in between) and passes under power cables. Follow the posts — each one bears a blue arrow, although some have been rubbed off by cows!

At the end of the second field go through the wooden gate into the wood. This is very pleasant and full of birdsong. On your left is a house called The Kennels. At the wood's end cross the unmade lane, go through the metal gate directly opposite and straight across the field. At the crest of the rise there is a lovely view across fields and trees.

Head towards the gate to your right at the edge of the woodland. It is marked with a blue arrow.

For the **shorter route,** go through the next gate on the right and follow the path through the wood, turning right at the end on to the quiet country road.

Stay on this (it bears sharp right at one point) until you arrive at the spot where you originally crossed to go through the double metal gates. Climb the stile on your left, marked with a yellow arrow, and head back towards Puddletown.

For the **longer route,** ignore the next gate on the right and walk along by the fence. You may well see hundreds of rabbits here (unless they see you first).

Climb the stile or go through the gate, then follow the line of the fence to the top of the hill, where you can admire the view at the next stile. Keep to the edge of the field and start watching out for a gate on the right into the wood. If you miss it you will come to a dead end, as we discovered by not paying attention to our map. The gate has a very faint blue arrow on it.

Once through the gate take the path to the left, which eventually leads to a gravel track with a house on the right. At the end turn right on to the road and proceed with care, as there is no verge.

Some way on you will see Duck Farm on your left. The smuggler George House lived in a cottage hereabouts when he was arrested for assaulting an Excise officer in 1791.

Between Norris Mill Farm and the next house, Higher Norris Mill, go through a gate on the right, marked with a yellow arrow, and cross the field, keeping to the fence. Look for a stile on the right and cross both this stile and a second one a few yards further on.

A little way on, cross another stile to the left, which is marked with a yellow arrow. You are now on Duddle Heath. The way is marked by yellow posts. Pass to the right of a tree with a yellow sign on it and then continue in the same way. At the edge of the woodland look for the yellow marker tree and follow the waymarkers through the forest.

At the stile is a "crossroads" of paths. Our route lies straight ahead, signposted Hardy's Cottage, but you may wish to stop and look at the pond on the left before proceeding. It is a haven for newts, dragonflies and other pondlife.

Follow the path to Hardy's Cottage. This is a pleasant wooded walk and it is not hard to imagine the smugglers' horses and wagons passing in convoy through these woodland paths 200 years ago, or the scene outside the cottage as they briefly broke their journey to offload some tubs of brandy for Thomas Hardy's grandfather to hide in his secret storeroom.

Keeping the Thomas Hardy Monument on your left, take the blue-marked bridlepath straight ahead — marked Puddletown on the wooden signpost.

Follow the main track, ignoring all paths to the side. The distant rumble of traffic can be heard to the left. This comes from the by-pass, out of sight beyond the trees.

On the other side of the by-pass lies Troy Town Farm, home of another suspected smuggler, John Knight, in 1813.

The track passes through woodland and across heath until it ends at a road junction.

Walk straight on, along the road facing you.

Keep walking until you meet the footpath used earlier on the walk. Rejoin the path opposite the double metal gates (a yellow arrow marks the way) and retrace your steps to Puddletown.

THE BATTLE OF MUDEFORD QUAY
Mudeford and Highcliffe Castle

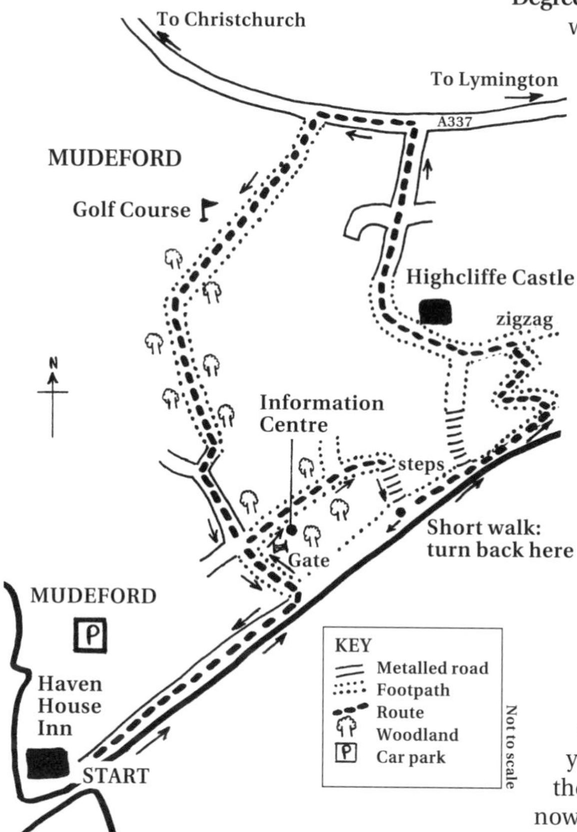

Degree of difficulty: An easy walk with excellent clifftop views. There is one long flight of steps but we have planned the route so that you go down them rather than up!

How to get there: Turn off the A35 Christchurch by-pass and follow the signs to Mudeford Quay.

Parking: Mudeford Quay has a large pay and display car park.

Pub facilities: The Haven House Inn on Mudeford Quay takes its name from its location at the entrance to Christchurch Harbour (or haven). Two hundred years ago the inn occupied the neighbouring building now known as the Dutch House and was a haven for smugglers, who took cover here during the Battle of Mudeford Quay (see History section). A more recent claim to fame is that the Haven House was the first pub in Britain to open all day on Sundays, since it was used for the official trial before the law was changed.

The pub is a free house, famous for its crab sandwiches and frequented by the local fishermen as well as visitors to this popular quayside location. Hot and cold

Distance: Longer walk approx 6 kms (4 miles); shorter walk approx 4 kms (2.5 miles).

Maps: OS Landranger 195 Bournemouth, Purbeck and surrounding area. Map ref: SZ 182 917.

Estate Publications red street plan (Bournemouth).

food and a wide range of bar snacks are always available. Children and wet suits are not allowed in the bar but the children at least are well catered for by the four outdoor terraces and the adjoining Haven Cafe which overlooks Christchurch Bay and the harbour entrance.

Opening times: Summer 11 am-11 pm Monday-Saturday, 12 noon-10.30 pm Sunday; winter 10.30 am-2.30 pm and 6-11 pm Monday-Friday, 12 noon-10.30 pm Sunday. Tel: 01425 272609.

Optional extras: A swimming costume, as you may be tempted to take a dip off Avon Beach or thereabouts. But beware of treacherous currents, which abound in this area. Consult maps and information boards for the safest spots.

Other attractions: There are **cafes and shops** at both Mudeford Quay and Avon Beach.

The **Information Centre** at Steamer Point Woodland is small, friendly and packed with treasures. Children will love it. A display of pebbles and driftwood has the rare and inviting label "Please touch"! A section has been painted by students taking the natural history illustration course at Bournemouth College of Art. The woodland scene incorporates doors which open to reveal a few surprises.

For those interested in the experimental radar dishes, which formerly stood near here, there is also a photograph taken before their removal. For details of children's pond puddling and other fun events, contact the warden on 01425 271262.

Highcliffe Castle, an ornate ruin built in the early 19th century, currently undergoing extensive restoration and open to the public.

The Haven House Inn, Mudeford

History: A visitor to Mudeford Quay 200 years ago would not have had to wait long to meet a smuggler. In these parts, the smuggling trade was part of everyday life and few people were not involved in it in one way or another. The most vivid account of the trade locally comes from a contemporary clergyman, the Rev Richard Warner, who described the number of smugglers in Christchurch and neighbouring villages as "immense". "It is," he wrote, "scarcely credible how many families were implicated more or less in this illicit and barbarising traffic; what large sums were accumulated by its practice; or with what openness and insolence it was carried on."

From their schoolroom above the chancel of Christchurch Priory in the late 1770s, the young Richard Warner and his friends used to watch the smugglers at work through a telescope. Many years later, he recalled: "I have, more than once, seen a procession of 20 or 30 wagons, loaded with kegs of spirits, an armed man sitting at the front and tail of each; and surrounded by a troop of 200 or 300 horsemen, every one carrying on his enormous saddle from two to four tubs of spirits; winding deliberately, and with the most picturesque and imposing effect, along the skirts of Hengistbury Head, in their way towards the wild country to the north-east of Christchurch, the point of their separation."

One of the Christchurch area smugglers named by Warner is "Slippery" Rogers, so-named from his "eel-like faculty for escaping the grasp of his maritime pursuers". Rogers's reputation was enhanced by the feats of his legendary ship, a speedy vessel of "extraordinary length and unequalled lightness", specially built for smuggling and manned by a daring crew who boasted of their preference for sailing in stormy weather. The ship had a long and successful smuggling career but her crew eventually defied the elements once too often and she was wrecked when approaching the coast with a cargo of contraband brought from Le Havre.

Another Christchurch smuggler – "a most notorious outlawed smuggler", to quote the official description – was John Streeter, who owned a tobacco and snuff factory at Stanpit and no doubt processed some of his illegal imports there. His ships included the *Civil Usage,* one of two smuggling luggers involved in Mudeford's most famous incident, the Battle of Mudeford Quay. This happened in July 1784 after the landing at Mudeford of two huge cargoes of spirits and tea by an army of 300 smugglers with 400 horses and 50 wagons. Such was the strength and arrogance of the smuggling gang that the crew of the *Swan* revenue cutter, who watched the whole operation, felt powerless to intervene. The goods were safely removed but next day the sloop of war Orestes came into the harbour. The smugglers, fearing the seizure of their luggers, ran both aground, removed the sails and materials, armed themselves and took cover behind a specially erected breastwork. When the Navy sent two tenders and several smaller boats alongside the luggers and demanded that the crews surrender, they were met by a volley of shots which wounded several men and killed the master of one of the tenders, 24-year-old William Allen, who was hit twice as he stepped ashore.

As the naval force continued its advance, guns blazing, the smugglers retreated to the Haven Inn, 300 or 400 yards away, and an adjoining stable. Amazingly, the gun battle continued for another three hours, wounding many on both sides. Eventually the naval and revenue men managed to capture both luggers and their longboats and towed them to Cowes on the Isle of Wight. A £200 reward was offered for information leading to the discovery of two or more of the offenders. Twenty-seven suspects were named in connection with the smuggling run, including John Streeter; warrants were issued against nine allegedly involved in the murder of William Allen. Of these, only three were arrested, and two of those acquitted, leaving a young smuggler called George Coombes to make the ultimate sacrifice on behalf of his many colleagues. Coombes was convicted of felony and murder, hanged at Execution Dock in London and his body hung in chains

Christchurch Harbour from Mudeford, where smugglers fought with the Royal Navy in 1784

near Christchurch Harbour until his friends cut him down and buried him.

The Walk: Before beginning the walk, take a couple of minutes to look around you and imagine Mudeford Quay before the days of motor cars and car parks and before it became a tourist attraction. It was little more than a seaswept spit then, as one visitor from Wimborne discovered in 1892. "The Haven consisted of two or three tumbledown Irish-looking houses on a narrow, sandy, flat peninsula with a bit of strap grass in the centre, sporting a few stunted pine trees and scraggy furze, surrounded by that diabolical invention barbed wire," noted Ernest J Brett.

Look at the Haven Inn and remember that it was here that smugglers took cover during a three-hour gun battle in 1784. Look back up the approach road to the car park and note the spot, 300 to 400 yards from the Haven Inn, where the smugglers ran their ships on to the harbour shore and began their spirited defence.

From Mudeford Quay, walk along the path by the sea wall in the direction of Highcliffe, passing Avon Beach cafe and shop. The beach stretches away towards Barton and Milford-on-Sea, offering a particularly good view of The Needles and the Isle of Wight. There is a map and information board by the beach office.

Walk past the beach huts and another cafe and when you reach the last hut – at the point where the promenade ends – take the path up the side of the slope to Steamer Point. The large concrete circles are the old footings of the experimental radar dishes which used to be here.

Turn right, go through the gate and head towards the woods along the track. There are seats facing out to sea and behind you is an excellent view of

Mudeford Quay and, in the background, Hengistbury Head

Mudeford Quay and Hengistbury Head. To the left lies the HM Coastguard Training Centre, just before the entrance to Steamer Point Woodland.

As you go into the trees, look out for the Information Centre on the right (see Other Attractions).

When you can tear yourself away from the information centre, go into the woodland, which is a thriving area of nest boxes and planting schemes. The ponds have viewing platforms and waterlilies.

Where the path divides, take the right fork and follow the route indicated by the "Beach via steps" sign. The steps are quite steep but the view makes it worthwhile.

For the **shorter walk,** turn right at the bottom of the steps and walk back along the beach to Mudeford Quay.

For the **longer walk,** turn left and walk across the pebbles past the steeply wooded cliff.

On reaching some wooden steps, the truly energetic walker can choose to climb them to the castle. The less energetic should walk a little further along the beach to take the more gentle zigzag path. At the top follow the gravel path to Highcliffe Castle (see Other Attractions and History).

From the castle, follow the road out of the car park, passing through the well-stocked gardens. Go straight along Rothesay Drive to the main road.

Turn left and walk along, past the golf clubhouse to the end of the pavement, where you will see a signpost to Steamer Point.

The tarmac path crosses the golf course and goes into the woods. When you reach some houses, follow the signs to the beach. Soon you will be back at the concrete circles.

From there follow the beach and promenade to return to the car park at Mudeford Quay.

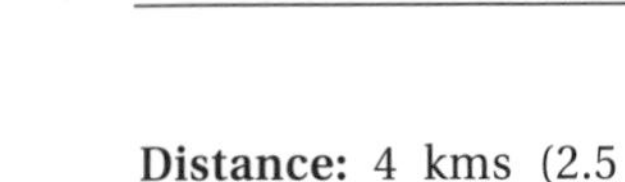

Walk No: 25

A FAMILY AFFAIR
Swyre

Distance: 4 kms (2.5 miles)

Maps: OS Landranger 194 Dorchester and surrounding area. Map ref: SY 528 882.

Degree of difficulty: This is a very pleasant walk in pretty countryside. Being particularly short, it is also ideal for a summer's evening stroll or for combining with a day trip to Weymouth or Abbotsbury.

It is an easy walk with a few stiles. But expect some mud especially in the final section.

How to get there: Swyre is on the B3157 between Bridport and Abbotsbury.

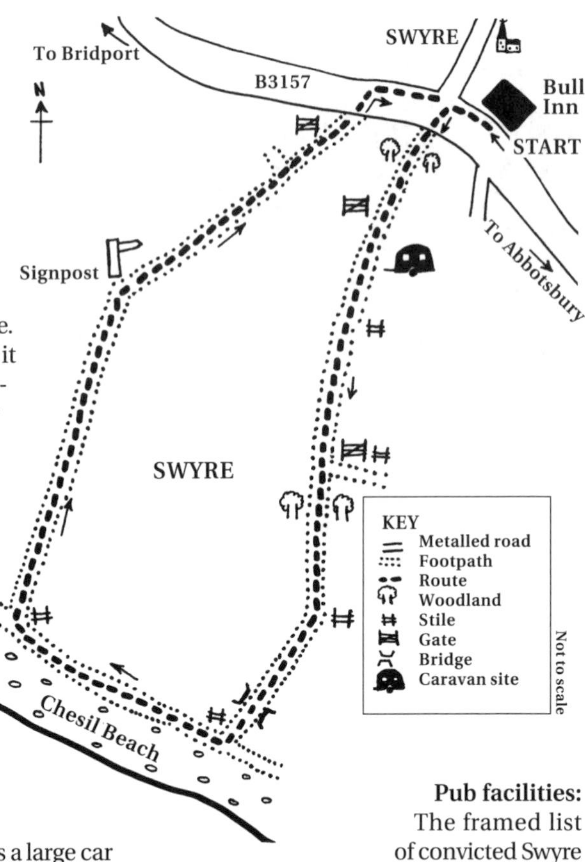

Parking: The Bull Inn has a large car park for patrons but it is often completely full in summer so walkers are not encouraged to park there except during the time that they are actually using the pub. There is, however, some roadside parking in the village.

Out of season, walkers intending to use the pub are invited to consult the licensees about parking. If trade is light and you "ask nicely", you may be allowed to use the pub car park.

Pub facilities: The framed list of convicted Swyre smugglers in the bar of **The Bull Inn and Restaurant** is reminder of this village's great smuggling heritage. The pub itself dates back to the 18th century (photographs on the wall show it in its former incarnation) but was completely rebuilt in 1939 and has been modernised since. It is now a free house serving morning coffee and a wide selection of meals and snacks as well as range of drinks which includes

The Bull Inn, Swyre

three real ales, three keg bitters, three ciders, two lagers, two stouts and a mild!

The Bull also has a children's room, small beer garden and children's play area with slide. Opening times: 10 am-3 pm or later and 6-11 pm Monday-Saturday, 12 noon-10.30 pm Sunday. Tel: 01308 897250.

History: Few Dorset villages were more heavily involved in smuggling than Swyre, and no Dorset family was more heavily implicated than the Northovers who lived there. In fact, of 22 smuggling prosecutions from Swyre in the surviving records of Lyme Regis Quarter Sessions and Dorchester Prison between 1725 and 1838, no less than 12 involved Northovers.

At Swyre, as elsewhere, smuggling was indeed a family affair, with skills, knowledge and contacts being handed down from father to son and son to grandson, just as in other trades and professions. Sometimes youngsters were introduced to the business at a very early age, as in the case of Charles Bishop, aged 13, who in 1835 was sentenced to six months imprisonment for smuggling. Of more than 800 smugglers listed in the records of Dorchester Prison over a 70-year period, Bishop was the youngest. The records describe him as a labourer and add that "this boy said his name was George Tomkins"!

Three years after Bishop's arrival in the county jail, one of his contemporaries, John Northover the Younger, aged 15, had his first taste of life behind bars. He was arrested on a charge of "making a fire as a signal to smugglers" but, unlike most of his forefathers, was found not guilty and released.

Other members of the Northover clan were involved in a serious incident at Swyre in 1825 as a result of which Joseph and James Northover and John Thorne alias Thornie alias Thorner were tried for assaulting the principal boatman of the Bridport Harbour Coastguard Sta-

Footprints in the shingle on Chesil beach

tion at West Bay. The following is taken from a contemporary newspaper report of Thorne's trial and is quoted verbatim to retain the flavour of the time:

"Grieg the boatman was examined and stated that himself and another boatman, being on duty at Swyre Gap about one in the morning on the 10th of March last, observed flashes about a mile to the eastward. They proceeded towards it, and saw a number of men carrying something on their backs from the beach path towards Puncknowle Hill. Witness and Eades proceeded towards the men, among whom were the prisoner and Joseph and James Northover. The whole party were armed with sticks and bludgeons, which they held in a threatening manner, frequently turning towards the witnesses; and James Northover threatened to kill him if he went any further. The prisoner at length jumped over the hedge and went away. Witness continued to pursue the others till he came to a stone wall, over which they had climbed: and as he was about to follow them he received a blow from Joseph Northover, which rendered him insensible for a short time. On coming to himself, he fired, and an officer hastened to his assistance, but the party had dispersed."

Thorne, who had been out of prison less than a year after serving 12 months for smuggling, was found guilty of obstruction but not guilty of assault. Joseph and James Northover were both found guilty of assault.

The Walk: On leaving the pub car park, turn right on to the main road. There is a pavement.

After a few yards, cross the road to take the footpath beside the war memorial. The path is indicated by a wooden signpost.

The path has bushes on each side. When you come to a gate go through it and walk down the field, keeping the fence on your right. There is a small caravan park on the left and the sea is visible straight ahead.

At the bottom of the field is a stile with a yellow arrow on it. Climb over and walk towards the gate and stile which you will see at the bottom of this field.

Having crossed the stile walk straight on. The path to the left floods in winter.

Keeping the hedge on your left, follow the track into a small copse.

The path emerges into a field. Walk along the left edge, in the shelter of the hedge.

Fishing from Chesil Beach

Keep the hedge on your left as you pass through a brambly section and walk down the slope to the edge of the next field.

Again keeping the hedge on your left, go to the next stile and climb over. It is marked with a yellow arrow.

Once over the stile, turn right and keep the hedge on your right.

Ahead is a wooden bridge. After crossing it, climb the stile immediately after it and you will be on the Chesil Beach.

The footpath runs along the back of the beach. The shingle falls in banks to the sea. There may be fishing boats to watch or a few anglers. This is not a bathing beach because of the steep shelving of the pebbles and the vicious currents.

After crossing the previously mentioned wooden bridge and stile at the back of the beach, turn right and head west. Behind lies Portland, and ahead is Golden Cap. On your left is the sea and to the right a sweep of farmland running to the crest of the hill.

After about a quarter-of-a-mile, cross the next stile and turn right, away from the sea. The path runs up the hill alongside a wooden fence on the right.

Halfway up the hill is a pillbox, a reminder of the last war.

At the top of the hill turn right, following the signpost which points to Swyre. This is a sheltered but sometimes muddy stretch between hedges.

Ignore the signpost pointing to Berwick on the left and go straight on.

There are views to the right over West Bexington and the sea. The main road is also visible, although unlike CS you will probably not encounter Ian Botham on his charity walk! At last the cheering was explained!

Walk through the gate at the top of the hill and turn right on to the main road just beyond it.

There is a short stretch without a pavement before you reach the war memorial where the walk began. Cross the road and head back to the pub.

THE END